Trends in Linguistics

Studies and Monographs

edited by

W. Winter

University of Kiel, Germany

1

Students and External Readers	Staff & Research Students
DATE DUE FOR RETURN	**DATE OF ISSUE**
23. DEC. 1986	-3 JUL 01 02951
30 JUN 1997	
	N.B. All books must be returned for the Annual Inspection in June

Any book which you borrow remains your responsibility
until the loan slip is cancelled

TAGMEMICS

Volume 1

ASPECTS OF THE FIELD

edited by

Ruth M. Brend

and

Kenneth L. Pike

1976

MOUTON

THE HAGUE - PARIS

ISBN 90 279 3425 0

Printed in the Netherlands

PREFACE

To the Two Companion Volumes on Tagmemics

In these two volumes we have endeavored to cover a number of the current theoretical concerns of tagmemicists by inviting persons who have actively contributed to various parts of the theory to write on them. Each author of the included chapters has published within the immediate past, one or more works on the areas he or she discusses and, in varying degrees, the chapter indicates the author's current thinking and gives some indication of his or her current and future research. The authors are not completely unified in their perspectives but, rather, show some of the varying views held by persons working with the theory.

These volumes, however, do not cover all of the areas currently being investigated by tagmemicists: for example, little mention is made of the application of mathematical group theory.[1] Also, although 'matrix' or 'field' theory is mentioned by several of the authors, its application to sub-morphemic constants is not covered at all.[2] In addition, the application of tagmemic theory to various peripheral areas such as music, psychotherapy, pedagogy, etc., is barely mentioned. Summaries of these and other areas of tagmemic research, not covered in these volumes may be found in publications of Viola Waterhouse,[3] Kenneth L. Pike,[4] and Ruth M. Brend.[5] And of course, details of work in progress by virtually all of the authors[6] have not been included.

Rather than a broad summary of all tagmemic research, therefore, we present here some of the results of tagmemic scholarship and some current directions of research, plus a considerable amount of theoretical discussion.

In the first volume, Robert Longacre (who himself has thus far been the inspirer and publisher of the majority of the tagmemic studies of discourse) summarizes the historical development of discourse analysis from the inception of the theory to the present, and he poses provocative questions regarding where the attention of scholars must now be placed. Eunice Pike gives a number of distinctive concepts of tagmemic phonology (to which she herself has contributed) and summarizes the research in this area. Mary Ruth Wise, in her chapter on language and behavior demonstrates that relationships between verbal and non-verbal behavior have been considered central to tagmemics and she summarizes the already extensive research on this topic, citing a wide range of publications.

vi

In the second volume, Peter Fries has organized his chapter around distinctions between surface versus underlying structure being made by a number of tagmemicists. He cites, in particular, publications related to this theme which describe syntactic levels below that of discourse. Austin Hale, whose training and earlier work has been chiefly as a transformational grammarian, discusses the place of rules and derivation within tagmemic theory and mentions some relationships between that theory and transformational grammar. Finally, Kenneth Pike presents some crucial tagmemic concepts, with a historical comment as to their inception and development, and then suggests a set of postulates to indicate some logical connections between those concepts.

The first volume, therefore, is largely a summary of language descriptions utilizing the theory, with a lesser amount of theoretical discussion than is found in the second volume. Together, however, these volumes present, we believe, a good summary of the state of some of the major areas of tagmemic research today.

Ruth M. Brend
Kenneth L. Pike
February, 1976

FOOTNOTES

1 See, for example, Kenneth L. Pike and Ivan Lowe, 'Pronominal Reference in English Conversation and Discourse: a Group Theoretical Treatment, ' *Folia Linguistica* 3, 68-106 (1969), and Ivan Lowe, 'An Algebraic Theory of English Pronominal Reference (Part I),' *Semiotica* 1, 397-421 (1969).
2 One of several publications in this area is by Kenneth Pike and Barbara Erickson Hollenbach, 'Conflated Field Structures in Potawatomi and in Arabic,' *International Journal of American Linguistics*, 30.201-212 (1964).
3 *The History and Development of Tagmemics*, The Hague: Mouton, (1974).
4 'A Guide to Publications Related to Tagmemic Theory,' *Current Trends in Linguistics* (ed. T. A. Sebeok) 3 The Hague: Mouton, pp. 365-94 (1966).
5 'Tagmemic theory: an Annotated Bibliography, (plus Appendix I),' *Journal of English Linguistics*, 4.7-45; 6.1-16. (1970, 1972).
6 For example a major pedagogical volume in preparation by Kenneth and Evelyn Pike to be published by the Summer Institute of Linguistics this year and a volume on discourse in preparation by Robert Longacre.

TABLE OF CONTENTS

DISCOURSE

R.E. LONGACRE
Summer Institute of Linguistics

This chapter is meant to be at the same time a historical sketch of the development of the analysis of discourse within tagmemics, a recounting of the accomplishments of such analysis, and a sketch of the contemporary scene and outlook in this regard. It is necessary first of all to note the linguistic scene in the early 1950's when tagmemics was getting under way. At the same time I note the initial emphases of early tagmemics and certain tensions within its framework. This brings us to a threshold year, 1958, which is of considerable importance to the development of the analysis of discourse within this tradition. Tagmemics at this time had taken on many of its present characteristics but was yet to feel the full brunt of the competition from transformational generative grammar which was in the ascendency – a competition which was both healthy and inevitable. Contemporary tagmemics has ended up considerably influenced by growing up in the same world in which transformational generative grammar was on the rise. Early applications of tagmemics to the analysis of discourse in languages of South America are discussed next. This brings us to another threshold year, 1964, characterized by certain crucial contributions of Pike to the study of discourse. It is also significantly the same year in which Gleason begins to publicly talk and write about the analysis of discourse within the framework of stratificational grammar. My own interest in discourse dates largely from the year 1965 with subsequent work in the Philippines and New Guinea, where I directed workshop programs in which the analysis of discourse was a focal consideration. Early in this same period Pike was also conducting similar workshops in Africa, and more recently in Nepal. Other contributions by various other tagmemicists (noticeably Wise, Klammer, and Becker) figure in the same period. The work of Joseph Grimes also dates from this time. Grimes, while not in the tagmemic tradition as such, has been influenced by it. His work however, will not be taken account of here because of the restriction of the scope of this article to discourse analysis within tagmemics proper. Suffice it to say that Grimes has conducted a series of highly successful workshops in different countries in which the analysis of discourse has been a focal consideration and in which there has been high productivity in terms of articles produced.

1. Tagmemics was first clearly adumbrated in a series of lectures by Pike to the staff of the Summer Institute of Linguistics at Norman, Oklahoma, in the summer of 1949. In these lectures Pike voiced the conviction that a slot-class unit, then called grameme, could provide a key to grammar just as the phoneme had provided the key to phonology. The term grameme was eventually changed to tagmeme under pressure from Bernard Bloch and others. Early tagmemics in this form including the term grameme is seen in the first volume of Pike's monumental work, *Language in relation to a unified theory of the structure of human behavior,* in the year 1954. What was the linguistic scene at this time (1949-54) and what did Pike fall heir to?

First of all, it is important to note that Pike, never narrowly parochial, had done his homework well. As an American structuralist, Pike had, in a brilliant decade of work, produced four significant works on phonology: *Phonetics* (1943), *The intonation of American English* (1945), *Phonemics* (1947), *Tone languages* (1948). Pike had known Sapir and Bloomfield personally and studied under them. He was never, however, an orthodox neo-Bloomfieldian or structuralist in that he resisted the emphasis on separation of levels. He, for example, never espoused juncture in the sense that it was espoused by Bloch, Trager, and Smith. Indeed as American linguistics increasingly hardened into a smug orthodoxy, Pike was one of the outstanding heretics of the era. Nevertheless as an heir of American structuralism, there were certain limitations in the viewpoint which Pike inherited which made for tensions in the framework of early tagmemics.

Pike was, however, a citizen of the world linguistically speaking. He was not content like so many American linguists of the period to ignore continental and British linguistics and go on his way preoccupied with the 'fun' that we were all having over here. He was for instance vitally interested in the work of J. Rupert Firth, of Louis Hjelmslev, and the Prague School, and was always pressing his colleagues to take account of contributions from these directions. What then did all this imply for the status of the study of discourse in early tagmemics?

As an heir of American structuralism, Pike did not receive much direct encouragement to study discourse. The attitude of Harris, however, towards the study of discourse was curiously ambivalent at this time. Harris's 1946 article "From morpheme to utterance" made it clear that by utterance, Harris intended sentence. Nevertheless, Harris had a significant section in that article called "stopping point". This is worth quoting: " one might ask how we can tell where to stop the analysis. This is answered by the nature of the work. All we do is to substitute one sequence for another in a given context. When

we have the formula for English utterances with assertion intonation, we find
that all we can substitute for it is another utterance with the same or another
intonation. When more work has been done on sentence sequences and what
is called stylistics, we may find that in certain positions within a sequence of
sentences, only N V /./, say, even occurs, to the exclusion of V /! /. When we
have such information, we will be able to extend the substitution procedure
to sentences and sequences of utterances (whether monologues or conversation)" (167-68). It is clear from this quotation that Harris did not envision any
necessary stopping at the sentence as a threshold, but envisioned the
possibility of continuing analysis right up through whole monologues and
conversation. His attitude seems to have been that we simply were not ready
to go in such a direction at the time that he wrote. By 1952, however, Harris
was working with what he called discourse analysis, which was an outgrowth
from the distributional analysis of descriptive linguistics, and which was at
the same time a variety of content analysis. At this point Harris confessed
that "...descriptive linguistics generally stops at sentence boundaries. This is
not due to any prior decision. The techniques of linguistics were constructed
to study a stretch of speech of whatever length, but in every language it
turns out that almost all the results lie within a relatively short stretch which
we may call a sentence."(1). He presented therefore his special methodology,
which he termed discourse analysis, which was to be the analysis of connected
speech, was to be formal, and was to be distributional. It was not a
generalized way to get at the grammar of discourse, but served rather to
reveal the content of a particular discourse, so that the structure of one
discourse was not expected to match the structure of other discourses. Harris
was able to say however, that his method "carries us past the sentence
limitation of descriptive linguistics"(2-3). He was further able to emphasize
"Language does not occur in stray words or sentences, but in connected
discourse — from a one word utterance to a ten volume work, from a
monologue to a union square argument. Arbitrary conglomerations of
sentences are indeed of no interest except as a check on grammatical
description, and it is not surprising that we cannot find inter-dependencies
among sentences of such an aggregate. The successive sentences of the
connected discourse offer fertile soil for the methods of descriptive
linguistics, since these methods study the relative distribution of elements
within a connected stretch of speech."(3). As an heir of American structuralism then, Pike inherited a method of description which generally did not
attempt to approach the structure of any unit higher than the sentence — and
which in effect was characterized by much more interest in morphology than
in syntax on the part of the average practitioner. At the same time, Zellig
Harris' interest in discourse reflected a certain dissatisfaction on the part of

4

one of the most prominent men on the current scene in this limitation of American structuralism to units no larger than the sentence.

Looking abroad, Pike found every reason to be interested in the study of discourse. Professor Vilém Mathesius (1892-1945), as founder of the Prague linguistic school, had had a long and fruitful academic career in which he had a persistent interest in matters of word order of English sentences as compared to Czech sentences. This interest of Professor Mathesius went back to Henri Veil's monograph *Ordre* published back in 1844, according to Professor Jan Firbas (1964b.111), Professor Mathesius' interest in word order in English and Czech compelled him to take account of contextual factors, and newness or oldness of information in context. These initial leads of Professor Mathesius are being followed up on the current scene by Professor Firbas and others as "functional sentence perspective". It is plain from a study of the contemporary writings of Firbas (1961, 1964a, 1964b, 1966, 1967) that we have here a very old and persistent interest in both verbal and situational context and in the communicative dynamism of discourse as it varies from sentence to sentence. The practitioner of functional sentence perspective is by definition one interested in the study of connected discourse.

The great Danish linguist, Hjelmslev, whose most important work was published in 1943 in Danish (but not until 1953 in English) was wholeheartedly committed to the study of what he termed *text* and what I would call discourse. As he says on page 9 of the English translation of his work, "The objects of linguistic theory are text." This is paraphrased again as "All conceivable or possible Danish texts" and is amplified on page 10 as "Any possible texts composed in any language whatsoever". His method, somewhat the opposite of Zellig Harris' "Morpheme to utterance" (1946), is to begin with a text and progressively partition it by various criteria of partitioning. Thus, he says: "The text is a chain and all of the parts (e.g. clauses, words, syllables) are likewise chains..." Analysis, he emphasizes, is a "constantly continued partition" (18). He says, furthermore, that analysis of partition is an accordian concept, i.e. we may blow up some given part of it and study that in depth in its own right.

The eminent British linguist, Firth, was similarly committed to the study of text. It is no accident that we find in some articles of Firth, extensive reference to and quotation from Hjelmslev with whom, however, he reserves the right to differ and whom he frequently criticises. The non-exclusion of meaning (as opposed to contemporary Americanist linguistics of his day) is vigorously defended by Firth, along with an emphasis on the study of the whole man in context, although he says that the special study of linguistics is linguistic text. These emphases are clear, e.g. in Firth 1951a. A further article of Firth's, "Modes of meaning" (1951b), has heavy emphasis on collocational and contextual meaning and extensive reference and partial analysis of literary works of Swinburne along with letters of Samuel Johnson and others, and literary works of Oscar Wilde. In his article "Structural linguistics" (1955), Firth again shows his indebtedness to not only Hjelmslev, but also to Mathesius of the Prague school. In brief, Pike had every encouragement from his European contemporaries and their immediate predecessors, to be interested in the study of discourse.

Before leaving this summary sketch of the linguistic scene when tagmemics was first getting under way, it is worth pausing to note what has happened to the various continental and British schools whose interest in discourse influenced Pike. I have already mentioned the Prague School where the study of discourse continues to be vigorously developed by Jan Firbas and others under the rubric "Functional sentence perspective". Hjelmslev's work has been crucial in the development of what is now called stratificational grammar. Stratificational grammar in turn has been highly productive of studies in the structure of discourse. As a practitioner of stratificational grammar, Gleason has seen several of his students produce monograph-length treatments of discourse in various languages. The work of J.R. Firth is continued by a variety of scholars, all loosely dubbed "neo-Firthian", but preserving a characteristically British independence of individual viewpoints. Among these especially noteworthy has been the interest of M.A.K. Halliday in discourse, as seen in his and Hasan's recent work (1973) "Cohesion and prominence in discourse".

2. Early tagmemics. 1954-7. In part 1 of *Language* (1954), Pike is seen to be profoundly interested in the structure of wholes. These wholes include not only whole texts and discourses, but behavioral complexes in which verbal and non-verbal behavior blend together and supplement each other. Thus he described a church service and a football game. Pike is so insistent on the importance of these wholes that he says (57): "The theory indicates that for adequate description and understanding one must start with some knowledge − even if crude or incomplete − of large units of behavior before studying smaller units within them." To serve his purpose, Pike sets up a unit which he calls the behavioreme, or "emic behavioral cycle". This is a large unit such as a church service or a football game, described in the same volume in detail − or even a family breakfast.

Focusing then on specifically verbal activities, Pike goes on to say (66) "We have illustrated at some length in this chapter, verbal behavioremes included within composite verbal-nonverbal ones; these verbal behavioremes we shall call utterence-emes or, with the term abbreviated for convenience, utteremes; utteremes constitute a subdivision of behavioremes, such that every uttereme is a behavioreme but not all behavioremes are utteremes. When we wish to distinguish between minimum behavioremes versus hyperbehavioremes, between small and large verbal types, we will speak of minimum utteremes and hyper-utteremes; one of the large conversation units (say the story mentioned above § 5.2) would be a variant of a hyper-uttereme; a single sentence would be a variant of a minimum uttereme." Pike goes on then to give criteria for the partitioning of a rather long hyper-uttereme into smaller units which would be smaller hyper-utteremes or simply minimum utteremes, i.e. sentences. Further on he discusses etic utterence types: jokes, limericks-parardies, puns, songs, cantatas, oratorios, presidential addresses, welcoming addresses, after-dinner speech, sermon, prayer, religious creed, slogan, proverb, epigram, conversation, a judge's giving sentence, and various sorts of sentences (69-70).

Still further on Pike has a section "on linguistic units larger than sentences". He begins this section (73-4) by observing that, "Linguistics in the past three decades made its most striking progress by dealing with units no larger than sentences" and goes on to admit that the study of structures larger than the sentence has largely been left to the students of literature. After paying his respects to a work of Jakobson and Lotz (1952), Pike takes account briefly of Harris' work called *Discourse analysis* (and mentioned earlier here). He feels that the work of Jakobson and Lotz is "much closer to the structure of the hyper-utterance, as we see it, than to the more widely-known recent attempt of Harris." He especially mentions Bloomfield's definition of sentence as an independent linguistic form and says that "It was perhaps this limitation which has prevented, in this country, the development of linguistics so that it would be integrated more closely with studies of literary form. When linguistic study deals with units larger than the sentence, a bridge may be built between linguistics and some kinds of literary study." At the end of this section he makes a plea for building on hyper-utterances, i.e. on whole discourses or texts. So much for Pike's undoubted interest in discourse from year one of the development of tagmemics.

But Pike's early definition of tagmeme (grameme) was somewhat inconsistent with his broader point of view. Defining a minimum utterance (to all intents and purposes an utterance as opposed to hyper-utterance) as sentence, Pike proceeded to chop his sentence into tagmemes, somewhat on the model of chopping an utterance into phonemes in phonology. Toward the end of part 1 (1954) he sets up a variety of 'utteremic-gramemic formulas' for various languagettes, i.e. small artificial language problems devised for pedagogical purposes. In this section it becomes very plain that tagmeme and uttereme of this sort are correlative concepts, so that essentially tagmeme is bounded by function within sentence and the sentence in turn is composed of tagmemes (I will not comment again on the fact that grameme in the period of 1954 is equivalent to tagmeme in subsequent work of Pike and other tagmemicists). This was a serious limitation and quite inconsistent with Pike's interest in wholes. It, for instance, meant that anything higher than the sentence had to be handled as something special, a hyper-utterance, while at the same time any internally complex structures below the sentence had to be handled as some kind of ad-hoc "subassembly" or something of the like, since tagmeme was correlative only to sentence-level formulas. The correlativity of sentence type and tagmeme was a built-in limitation which had to be disposed of before tagmemics could continue to develop in the direction of analysis of units larger than the sentence, and for that matter, of units smaller than the sentence. This brings us to an important threshold year, 1958.

3. With the year 1958, tagmemics enters into a new period of development. This was the year in which I was able to influence Pike in the direction of abandoning the correlativity of tagmeme and utterance for a tagmeme relative to any given level of structure, from stem on up to discourse itself. Quite as important − possibly of greater importance − was an unpublished article of Jim Loriot's concerning Shipibo paragraph structure.

Pike had in the 1954 work posited a unit, hyper-grameme (or hyper-tagmeme) which was characterized as a sequence of two tagmemes both of which were obligatory, i.e. a +A +B structure. I suggested that hyper-tagmemes of this sort be redefined so as to include any structurally contrastive string type, e.g. a word type, a phrase type, a clause type, a sentence type, regardless of whether it be composed of +A +B units or +A ±B, etc., units. Calling this unit at first hyper-tagmeme after Pike, I eventually, following Waterhouse (and with an even older cue from de Saussure), decided to call the unit *syntagmeme* (Waterhouse 1958 dissertation; published in 1962). This yielded tagmeme and syntagmeme as correlative concepts, i.e. syntagmemes are composed of tagmemes and tagmemes are slots which are filled by syntagmemes. Much of this remained to be worked out and has been worked out subsequently (cf. Longacre 1960, 1965, 1970a). Nevertheless a beginning of this sort made possible a symmetric and parallel handling of any type of structure from a combination of roots (which constitutes a stem) or a stem plus inflectional affixes (which constitutes a word) on up to consideration of discourse itself. We could now have not only sentence-level tagmemes, but paragraph-level and even discourse-level tagmemes. This broke a termino-logical and perhaps a conceptual log-jam in early tagmemics and brought these definitions into better accord with the main thrust of Pike's work, paving the way for systematic exploration of the units higher than the sentence.

Meanwhile, a younger colleague of ours, James Loriot of Peru, raised in the jungles and educated by correspondence courses, came out with a truly remarkable accomplishment in the year 1958. Using the slot-class technique of tagmemics (but acknowledging a certain debt to Hjelmslev and others), Loriot explored paragraph structure in Shipibo of Peru, which he had learned to speak as a youngster. This paper has had a profound influence on discourse analysis within tagmemics from the year in which it was written to the present time. It is unfortunate that it remained unpublished until the year 1970 when it appeared as a paper joint-authored with Barbara Hollenbach. Quoting from the 1970 article can be rather misleading, however, because it is always problematic as to how much subsequent developments may influence the phraseology of an early paper whose publication is delayed for many years. The crucial contribution is clear, however. Loriot wrote his paper in a day when grammar was considered to stop with the sentence and where Harris' discourse analysis was some kind of special aberrant development. Loriot didn't stop there. He didn't hesitate to go beyond the domain of individual sentences and find grammatical ties across sentence boundaries. And he was convinced that he was dealing with structure and not with fortuitous overlapping phenomena in a series of sentences.

Especially important in studying this paper is noticing how the mass of detail was handled. Description of this mass of detail is handled under three heads: "Tactical structure of texts", "Event-reference ties", and "Object-reference ties". Under the first head Loriot discusses two conjunctions, both loosely translated 'thereupon', to serve as paragraph introducers. Then he goes on to consider words and classes of words which introduce various slots within the paragraph. He further discussed the use of present and past participles within the paragraph framework, as well as various tenses and modes of verbs, pronoun versus noun (in pronominalization chains), and the distribution of various classes of verbs such as phasals (beginning and ending), transforms (becomes), statives, motion verbs, expression verbs (verbs of speech), and intransitive action verbs. Especially interesting I find his reference to "chains of clauses with past participial overlap." He explains: "This overlap is often accomplished by the use of past participles introducing each new clause summarizing the action of the previous clause" (57). He also mentions the conjunction *jaibi* as a marker of frustration within the paragraph. All these varied phenomena are discussed in relation to the paragraph as a unit. Under the second head, event-reference, he discusses antonyms and paronyms (i.e. two verbs referring to the same event), and gives conditions and rules for recognition of, and use of, paronyms. One class of paronyms which he refers to, which I have found in my own studies to be significant, is negated antonym, i.e. 'not black but white'. For object-reference, after briefly discussing ties to the real world, he discusses matters of linguistic antecedents and anaphora. Of special interest here is the matter of "ties between items in narrative and items in quotation embedded with the narrative." (61). Rules are given for pronominal reference for pronouns used as subject and pronouns used as object. Then ties and breaks within a clause are given as well as ties and breaks across clauses and anaphora involving possession reference.

The effect of my work in revising the framework of early tagmemics was immediately felt in two directions. One was in the Part III of Pike's *Language* (1960). Here the revision was frankly accepted although with the due amount of inspection and comment which one would expect in a thinker of the originality and depth of Pike. Pike baptized a tagmeme of the sort which I now envisioned as "relative level tagmeme", discussed its pros and cons, but as a whole accepted the revision. Secondly, the influence of my work was seen in Velma Pickett's monograph *The grammatical hierarchy of Isthmus Zapotec.*. Both of these works came out in the year 1960. Pickett sets up as various hierarchical levels the following: word, phrase, clause, sentence, utterance, and discourse. The latter two are a source of some confusion. Utterance is defined as the stretch between when a single speaker begins and stops talking. Since discourse is defined as either monologue or conversation, utterance can therefore be smaller than discourse. But in many respects independent utterance equals discourse in her framework. She spoke of narrative episode, sermon, instruction, soliloquy, exclamation, as types of utterances, and then she went on to say "monologue discourse types overlap with utterance level structures and that at this point utterance equals discourse" (13). Never-theless – and this is the important point – Pickett's work showed the complete correlativity of tagmeme and syntagmeme on the various levels of structure.

The impact of Loriot's work was especially felt in the study of various South American Indian languages in the years after 1958. Thus Eugene Loos (1961) in his "Capanahua narrative structure" acknowledges frankly his debt to Loriot and discusses paragraph markers, topic of the paragraph, and linkages between sentences. Powlison, in an article written in 1963 but not published until 1965, also acknowledged his debt to Loriot in the following words "Some of my first notions of how to proceed on paragraph analysis were gained from James Loriot and his unpublished manuscript, "Shipibo Paragraph Structure" (1958)". Powlison posited paragraphs with two layers of recursion within the paragraph, as Loriot had also posited a certain amount of recursion on the paragraph level in his work as well. In chopping a discourse into paragraphs, Powlison took account of the following features:

1) Initially paragraphs were set up by reference to phonological clues; 2) in positing onset of a new paragraph, Powlison looked for "spotlight on a character entering the story"; 3) a paragraph was a chain of stimulus responses, i.e. somewhat of a dramatic dialogue, in that a Yagua folktale employs characteristically a lot of dialogue in its development; 4) there is a pattern of characteristic slots which constitute a paragraph (action, reason, consequent action, reason$_2$); and finally 5) there is frequent occurrence of paragraph setting in paragraph initial, with paragraph setting involving things like time, location, direction, and situation. Powlison also observed that the *core* of a paragraph could be recognized as a structure consisting of a verb with the emphatic suffix.

Meanwhile, Gudschinsky, who like the rest of us was initially stimulated to study discourse by Loriot's unpublished article, was serving as linguistic consultant to Summer Institute of Linguistics personnel in Brazil for the years 1959-1963. Gudschinsky found in her consultant work on various languages of that country, that clause level tagmemes indicating time and location were loosely being indicated as optional within the clauses in which they occurred while, in fact, in regard to the structure of larger units such as paragraph and discourse, they were anything but optional. In fact their distribution could be quite neatly predicted. Under her influence a great deal of research was done although unfortunately most of this research is either unpublished or in very obscure and difficult-to-obtain outlets. Nevertheless, Derbyshire on Hixkaryana, Taylor on Kaiwa, Harrison on Asurini, Huestis on Bororo, Popovich on Maxakali, and Majory Crofts on Munduruku, all made contributions to the understanding of units higher than the sentence within discourse.

I would judge that Harold Popovich's article (1967) is indicative of the type of contribution made at this time. It is brief but exciting. It recounts that after Maxakali clauses had been analyzed, several problems remained. "These problems involve the use of motion verbs, the use of conjunctions, the distribution of simple time phrases versus time phrases included in clauses. Oddly enough, all the problems seem to refer to time or space. We hypothesize that temporals and locationals might be the defining features of paragraphs." These problems proved to be severe and unsolvable without some reference to some unit higher than the clause-sentence itself, so the paragraph unit was posited. Positing a paragraph, the problem of use of the motion verbs 'come' and 'go' was solved. It was necessary to assume that the spatial setting of a paragraph involved three possible areas, a home area, places in passing, and an area of travel between these — which were called by Popovich, nuclear, marginal, and transitional areas respectively. Motion toward the nuclear area was indicated with the verb 'come' and motion away from the nuclear area was indicated with the morpheme 'go'. In addition there were three conjunctions all loosely translated 'and', one of which was used with the nuclear area, the other with the marginal area, and the other with transition from the nuclear area or from the basic temporal settings to the specific time segment of the next clause. In reference to the paragraph unit it was found that a time phrase which occurs outside of the (initial) clause, indicated the time setting for the entire paragraph while the time phrase within the clause indicated the setting only of the action indicated in that clause itself. The final paragraph of Popovich's article eloquently summarizes the findings: "The time and space settings are interrelated. Each narrative paragraph contains either one spatial or one temporal setting or both of these. The temporal setting occurs at the very beginning of the paragraph. The nuclear area of the spatial setting occurs anywhere in the first half of the paragraph. If both settings occur, the temporal setting precedes the nuclear area. If either set does not occur it is understood to be the same as the preceding paragraph."

The Maxakali article and other articles from the same period illustrate well the problems encountered in trying to analyze South American Indian languages within the restricted domain of the sentence. Grammatical features of importance can be understood only by reference to units larger than the sentence. Here, if nowhere else in the world, the limitations of a sentence grammar were easily seen.

Also from the same period is an article by Gudschinsky herself (1968). The title rendered in English is "A tagmemic analysis of the units which combine verbal and nonverbal components." Here Gudschinsky proceeded in the grand tradition of Pike in volume 1 of his *Language*. Her article gives documentation of dialogue-like exchanges in which nonverbal components are an essential part of the exchange.

Reflecting work of the same period but not complete until 1966 is Loraine Bridgeman's monograph *Oral paragraphs in Kaiwa*. Bridgeman's work deserves more attention than it has attracted to date. It is a careful attempt to take Pike's trimodal structure seriously. It investigates phonological, grammatical, and lexical paragraphs in Kaiwa, showing that paragraphs in the various modes of structure do not necessarily prove to be congruent. Analysis of phonological paragraphs is an application of high-level phonology which has a long tradition in tagmemics. (See the contribution of Eunice V. Pike elsewhere in this volume.) Her work on grammatical paragraphs is somewhat run of the mill for this time in which it is written. Her work on lexical paragraphs is truly unusual and deserves careful examination. She proceeded in setting up lexical paragraphs to notice features of comparative lexical density or scatter within a paragraph. Are several key lexical items introduced

12

early in the paragraph and repeated constantly, or do we find a comparative paucity of lexical items early in the paragraph and a comparative abundance of lexical items later on? Do we find a narrowing, a broadening or a narrowing-broadening of the lexical content? By such means she was able to think of paragraphs as having, roughly speaking, geometric shapes — rectangular paragraphs, triangular-shaped paragraphs with the shape of an equilateral triangle whose apex is up versus similar paragraphs like a triangle whose apex is down, an hour-glass-shaped paragraph or conversely, paragraphs which bulge at the center, etc. Here is where application of Harris' discourse level analysis, i.e. content analysis, can be made to serve as the handmaiden of linguistics to obtain lexical paragraphs in which we are concerned wholly with matters of content and not with matters of grammatical structure whether superficial or deep. I believe that Bridgeman has given us some valid clues in this direction which nobody has to date followed up.

Toward the end of this intermediate period of development within tagmemics, comes an article by V. Waterhouse, "Independent and Dependent Sentences" (1963). Pike had mentioned Bloomfield's definition of sentence as a persistent hang-up within American structuralism. Waterhouse proceeded to elaborate somewhat more vigorously as follows: "Where sentences are concerned, however, the Bloomfield definition that 'each sentence is an independent linguistic form, not included by virtue of any grammatical construction in any larger linguistic form' seems to have the status of the law of the Medes and the Persians. This has resulted in an atomistic pre-occupation with units no larger than the sentence by scholars from Bloomfield all the way to exponents of transform grammar". After this Waterhouse refers in the same article to "recent analysis in some aboriginal languages" which shows that "some sentences are independent and therefore to be included in some larger linguistic form such as paragraph and discourse" (45). At this point Waterhouse also refers to Loriot's unpublished manuscript on Shipibo paragraph structure. Waterhouse then proceeds to set up a square matrix in two parameters, dependent versus independent, and complete versus incomplete which she illustrates in the following fashion: Dependent complete, i.e. sentences such as *Consequently there is no water left in the well*; Dependent incomplete, i.e. such sentences as *But not now!*; Independent complete sentences such as *Jack threw the ball straight at Susie*; and Independent incomplete sentences such as *Just got back from Austin yesterday*. She classifies dependent sentences as sequential sentences, i.e. sentences beginning with such conjunctions as *hence, and so, similarly, therefore, besides, for, in addition to*, etc.; referential sentences which involve third person pronouns and pro-verbs such as *I honestly would, we all do*, etc.; and completed sentences which are essentially responses, not necessarily answers to questions, but responses to comments and continuations of previous conversations. The article is an instructive ensemble of examples from her corpus of English and should be of interest to any student of English paragraph and discourse structure whatever the framework of reference in which he is working. At the end of the article, Waterhouse broadens its scope to include other examples from various languages of Mexico and Peru: Campa, Chontal of Oaxaca, Isthmus Zapotec, Tzeltal, Huitoto, Zoque, and Iquito.

While tagmemics was steadily moving in the direction of greater and greater attention to the analysis of connected discourse, transformational-generative grammar, rising steadily towards a position of dominance in the linguistic departments in most institutions within the United States, was not only failing to interest itself in analysis of units larger than the sentence, but was somewhat perversely defining grammar in terms of its low-level focus. Thus, the first generation of transformational-generative grammarians defined grammar as a set of rules for generating all (and only) well-formed sentences within a given language, thus automatically labeling itself as a system of sentence grammar, as opposed to discourse grammar. Katz and Fodor (1964: 173) went out on the end of a long limb − which visibly cracked under them − when they wrote "Grammars seek to describe the structure of a sentence *in isolation from its possible settings in linguistic discourse (written or verbal) or in nonlinguistic context (social or physical)."* Fortunately a subsequently awakened interest in discourse structure has rescued transformational-generative grammar from this impossible posture in which it found itself at this early period. Robin Lakoff's recent interest in discourse structure (1972) and the interest of van Dijk (1972) and Petöfi (1971, 1972a, 1972b) in Europe are indicative of a very sophisticated treatment of discourse from the standpoint of transformational-generative grammar. Both latter scholars admit freely the limitations of a sentence-oriented grammar and plead eloquently for discourse grammar.

But this is somewhat ahead of our story which has thus far progressed no further than the early 1960's, and in which we have been building up to another threshold year − 1964.

4. 1964 is characterized by two important pieces of writing on the part of Pike. One is his classic little article "Beyond the sentence" (reprinted in Brend, 1972). Here Pike makes the following bold unequivocal statement: "A bias of mine − not shared by many linguists − is the conviction that *beyond the sentence* lie grammatical structures available to linguistic analysis, describable by technical procedures, and usable by the author for the generation of literary work through which he reports to us his observations... sheer delight

awaits the linguist who sees the poem as linguistically a unique lexical event (an intricate "idiom" as it were) with an interlocking (partially unique) phonological structure embedded in a high level grammatical pattern (in a genre, that is to say), which is in part determined culturally and in part created newly." (Brend 1972. 192). The same article shows Pike's interest in jokes and puns and insists on various connections with poetry. A poem of Emily Dickenson's, "The brain within its groove" is analyzed. Pike winds up at the end on a becoming note of humility: "Just as no one complete success has ever been achieved in devising a mechanical procedure to *analyze* a novel or sentence, so also we must not built our hopes on any mechanical procedure to *generate* all possible useful and *beautiful* sentences and sonnets... beyond the linguist lives the artist." (Brend 1972. 199).

Also in the same year (1964) Pike had finished his revision of the three-volume work, *Language in relation to a unified theory of the structure of human behavior,* which appeared as one volume in 1967. In this republished volume, Pike substitutes for the section "on linguistic units larger than the sentence", a much more strongly worded paragraph or two. The comparison of the earlier paragraph (Part I 1954.73-4) with the later paragraphs, shows a certain progress in Pike's thinking. Although he had faced in this direction in 1954, he was prepared in 1964 to express himself more vigorously: "Our view, on the other hand, continues to be (as in the first edition of this book, 1954) that the sentence is a totally inadequate starting or ending point. Sentences themselves cannot be analyzed without reference to higher level relationships." (1960.147, cf. whole section 145-8)

It is of interest that in this same year, 1964, Gleason read a paper at a Georgetown Roundtable in which he expressed his view as follows: "I recently put together a rough sketch of a stratificational grammar of a non-European language [Kate of New Guinea]. My objective, at first, was the quite traditional one of generating sentences, and I was able to do at least as satisfactorily as in any of a number of previous attempts in a variety of models. Then quite by accident, I discovered that the grammar would cover whole narratives as well as single sentences. Less had to be added to expand the coverage than could be deleted as no longer required. In this language the stratificational grammar of whole narratives seems to be actually simpler than that of sentences abstracted from narrative and examined separately... after all, a narrative is a much more natural unit of language than is the sentence. Native speakers produce narratives with ease." (Gleason 1964.94)

I quote Gleason above as a rather striking coincidence with Pike's own work in the same year. Both men were expressing themselves with increasing positiveness that the sentence analyzed in isolation from discourse produced a very unsatisfactory analysis. It reminds me of some advice that I received in theological seminary, where as a homiletic student, I was taught in reference to the exegesis of Scripture that "a text without a context is a pretext", (where the word *text* refers to a particular scripture passage instead of to a whole discourse as it does in contemporary parlance). But verses of Scripture cannot be understood outside their context precisely because verses of Scripture occur within connected discourse. At this point the limitations of Scriptural exegesis are the limitations of the understanding of any sentence in any context anywhere.

From the same period date contributions of two colleagues of Pike at the University of Michigan, Alton L. Becker and Richard E. Young. The two collaborated in an article, "The role of lexical and grammatical cues in paragraph recognition" (1964) and in a further joint article, "Toward a modern theory of rhetoric: a tagmemic contribution" (1965). Becker wrote two further articles on the paragraph: "A tagmemic approach analysis" (1965) and "Symposium on the paragraph" (1966). All this eventually led to a joint work by Young, Becker and Pike, *Rhetoric: Discovery and change,* (1970). In this volume results of tagmemic study, including attention to discourse, are assembled in an attempt to guide students in the appreciation of literature and in the attaining of a more satisfactory style in composition.

Also from Pike's pen in the year 1964 is an article "Discourse analysis and tagmeme matrices" in which Pike shows an interest in underlying role structures (actor, undergoer, etc.) as they move in and out of surface-structure slots within a discourse. This article grew out of a workshop of Pike's in the Philippines in the year 1962-1963 in which an embryonic form of case grammar was evolved as necessary to the description of Philippine languages. The year 1965 saw further developments in the tagmemic analysis of discourse. I was privileged that year to direct a workshop in Mexico with three research workers studying the same language, Totonac. I was able to put one worker, Aileen Reed, on the analysis of clause, her colleague, Ruth Bishop, on the analysis of sentence structures, and still a third colleague, Ella Button, on the analysis of paragraph and discourse. This was an unusual opportunity. The three-pronged attack on the same language, each by a person able to speak the language and in consultation with the others, provided for a very unusual research situation. Out of it grew a monograph (1968) in which I figured as the fourth author, ghost writer, and general editor. The title of the volume, "Totonac: from clause to discourse", is itself significant. As I wrote in the introduction "The title of this volume is indicative of the belief of its authors that grammar does not cease above the sentence level but extends on up through paragraph and discourse. A language is a consistent whole. Certain features of word and clause structure find their ultimate rationale only by reference to higher levels which include and go beyond the sentence. Furthermore, sequences above the sentence may be shown to have grammatical structure in no essential way different from that found on lower levels. In the process, however, the notion of sentence itself — that level medianly spaced between the linguistic stratosphere and troposphere — must be brought into better focus." (11). Note especially in the above quote that the claim is stubbornly made that grammar above the sentence differs in no appreciable way from grammar below the sentence. This is not a popular position. Even linguists such as Gleason and Halliday, who believe in grammar above the sentence, hedge their belief with remarks to the effect that constituent structure of the sort found in the clause and below it is not found further upward. Gleason says that above the clause-sentence we settle for network structures. My experience in the Totonac workshop was, however, that tree structures of discourse and paragraph were just as plausible as tree structures of sentences and clauses; that formulas could be compiled for discourse and paragraph just as formulas could be compiled for sentence and clause; and that there seemed to be no reason to assume a discontinuity of structure above the sentence itself.

As indicated, however, in the quotation from my introduction to the Totonac volume, the sentence itself had to be brought into better focus. This we attempted to do with some success in the Totonac volume itself and in subsequent work. Too often clause and sentence are used somewhat interchangeable by contemporary linguists. Often the term sentence in effect is used to mean the one-clause sentence. In fact the study of discourse probably starts with any unit above the clause, i.e. sentence, paragraph, and discourse units — not to mention features of clause, phrase, and word which are influenced by discourse structure. It has therefore been somewhat difficult to bound the scope of this chapter. But I have tried to concentrate mainly on paragraph and discourse although there has had to be some attention to the sentence itself. In this respect my contribution overlaps a bit with that of Peter Fries in the companion volume of the present one.

In the year 1965-1966, Pike held linguistic workshops in Ghana and Nigeria, West Africa. As a whole, the workshops did not concentrate on the paragraph and discourse levels, but there is a significant chapter in Pike's report volume (1966) called "Beyond the sentence". This chapter (52-62), that presents preliminary evidence for a paragraph level in West African languages. The evidence is drawn from the work of Marjory Crouch on Vagala. Pike argues that there is formal marking of a primary independent sentence versus a secondary sentence which follows it. The marking is via a complicated contrastive pattern of tone differences, occasionally supplemented by certain suffixes. Pike argues that granted the first point, we must then show that "the second element of this sequence is indeed a sentence and not merely a clause". The argument is rounded out by showing that an independent sentence may be followed by several dependent sentences, and that the resulting unit, larger than a single sentence, has semantic plausibility. This is of interest here in that we have, in effect, paragraphs not set up in somewhat oblique fashion as in English but posited on the basis of a formal marking of the unit. As to the semantics involved, Pike says they could all be given a general structure of *proclamation* versus *commentary*. But this is broken down into more specific relations such as command plus carrying out of a command, request plus carrying out of request, statement of intent plus carrying out of intent, and principal action-initiating-sequence-of-action plus subsequent action. The first three, i.e. command, request, or statement of intent — plus fulfillment — are very similar to what we have subsequently called execution paragraphs in the Philippines and in New Guinea. The fourth relation which Pike mentions, a sequence of actions plus a subsequent action, appears to be nearer to the run-of-the-mill narrative paragraph, which is found in most languages, plus a result of the last action.

In the remainder of this chapter Pike writes of direct and indirect quotations and how general discourse constraints dictate the choice of one versus the other. This grew out of some very practical considerations in the translation of portions of the New Testament into West African languages, and preaching and teaching in those languages. Certain missionary personnel were occasionally appalled to find that when they told their audience, "Jesus said, 'I am the light of the world' ", the audience said, "Oh, fine, so Jesus says that you are the light of the world." Evidently, what the missionary had hoped to give as a direct quote, i.e. "Jesus said, 'I am the light of the world. '" was taken as an indirect quote, "Jesus says that I am the light of the world" — and thus referred to the speaker herself. On investigation the selection of indirect and direct quotations was found to be a highly sensitive pattern involving discourse-level constraints (especially for the Bariba language, data provided by Jean Soutar). It is significant here that from this time on, Pike acquired an interest in the structure of direct and indirect discourse, culminating eventually in his joint work with Ivan Lowe. In this work Pike and Lowe were able to apply group theory to pronominal reference involving the reporter himself, people whose speech is reported within the quotation, and third parties (Pike and Lowe, 1969).

5. In the years 1967-68, I held linguistic workshops in the Philippines and during the year 1970 a similar series of workshops in New Guinea. In both workshop programs (under the sponsorship of the Office of Education) specific attention was given to sentence, paragraph, and discourse. The resulting report volumes (Longacre 1968, 1972a) contain various items of

interest to the general student of language in spite of the fact that the regional names in their titles seem to indicate preoccupation with certain linguistic areas of the world to the exclusion of others. I therefore summarize somewhat at length the results of these two projects.

In the Philippines workshop program (OE contract # 0-8-062838-0391) I was in an enviable position as principal investigator. Twenty-five related languages were under study with personnel who had lengthy experience living among the peoples of the folk cultures involved, and who had learned to speak their languages. Furthermore, many of the people involved in the workshop programs had already done creditable work in the phonemics, morphology, and clause structure of the languages represented. My job was to direct the attention of these people to areas of research that they had not contemplated before, namely discourse, paragraph, and sentence structures, in the languages which they were studying. Something like a chain reaction of discovery ensued. From the foment emerged 1) a theory of discourse genre and of the devices for linking paragraphs and embedded discourse together to form discourses in these various genres; 2) a theory of paragraph types and of the devices for linking sentence with sentence and embedded paragraph with embedded paragraph within such paragraphs; 3) a theory of dialogue and of dramatic discourse; 4) an opportunity to catalogue and compare sentence types and sentence systems in a variety of related languages and thereby obtain a better idea of the range and variety of sentence structure within a typical group of languages; 5) an attempt to push situational or 'lexical' structure on up into the paragraph and discourse levels.

In positing discourse genre within the Philippine languages studied, we were driven again and again to take account of the total framework of a discourse and of the way that its parts go together rather than to the basic sort of material found within it. Thus, as I describe in the Philippine report volume (1968.1.10), there is a Maranao narrative discourse (from Robert Ward) which does not contain a single narrative paragraph. By what rights is such a discourse called a narrative discourse when all of its paragraphs are expository paragraphs? The reason is not hard to state. The seven paragraphs constitute an embedded narrative discourse for the sole and compelling reason that they are joined in chronological sequence, i.e. each of the seven successive paragraphs describes a situation on a given chronological horizon subsequent to that of the previous paragraph. The discourse is about the sufferings of the Muslim faithful in the Soviet Union at the hands of the communists. The first paragraph of the discourse begins "When the Bolshiviks first came to power in 1917". The next paragraph continues "During the next ten years". The next paragraph says "In the second World War," etc. This example is instructive of the fact that in considering discourse genre and assigning a given example to a given genre we do not look fundamentally at the sort of content found in a discourse but at its overall framework and how its parts link together.

Five main discourse genres were distinguished in the Philippines project. Of these, four constitute a system with systemic parameters, one parameter of which is succession with plus and minus values and the other of which is projected time with plus and minus values. Narrative discourse is that discourse which is plus (chronological) succession and minus projected time i.e. the events are considered to have already occurred. Procedural or how-to-do-it discourse is that discourse genre which is plus succession and plus projected time, i.e. it is assumed that this is how it would be done whenever one were in the mood to do it or whenever conditions called for one's doing it. Expository discourse is that discourse genre which is minus succession and minus projected time, i.e. expository discourse neither involves chronological succession nor consideration of time at all; it simply explains a subject matter. Hortatory discourse is that discourse which is minus succession and plus projected time. Hortatory discourse is discourse aimed at influencing conduct. It does not involve chronological succession but it does involve an element of projection, i.e. this is how one is to act whenever one finds himself in certain situations.

The four discourse genres were also distinguished as to certain subordinate parameters. Person orientation is such a parameter. Narrative discourse is commonly told in first or third person. There are, of course, several varieties of third person discourse and probably more than one variety of first person account as well. Narrative discourse in second person is somewhat novel and rare. It is typically a trick of Western culture ("This is a story of your life..."). Procedural discourse may be told in any person in the surface structure; in the underlying structure it is essentially non-specific as to person while narrative discourse is specific as to person. The non-specific character of procedural discourse coincides with its being in projected time, i.e. the time is not past or real and the people involved in it in this sense are not past or real but are simply typical participants. Expository discourse has no particular person orientation. It is subject-matter oriented, and is typically in the third person but first and second-person may come in the "I am explaining to you" situation. Hortatory discourse has an underlying second person component regardless of how this is expressed in the surface structure, i.e. the surface structure can say *you should do this* or can say *we do this* or *we don't do this* meaning 'this is what you should do' or can say, *a good x does so and so* where x can signify, e.g., an American or Australian or Frenchman (meaning 'you as an American or Australian or Frenchman should act as follows').

Another subordinate parameter is linkage mechanisms. Narrative and procedural discourse have chronological linkage, while expository and hortatory discourse have logical linkage. Within the context of a given Philippine language we find characteristic linkage devices differing for all four. But this must be stated in terms of the surface structure of a given language.

Outside this system and in addition to it is dramatic discourse. Dramatic discourse could be thought of as consisting of quotation sentences with deleted quotation formulas. But this would be a work of supererogation. Rather than considering that there has been wholesale deletion of quotation formulas from quotation sentences in order to form dramatic discourse, it is better to consider that such quotation formulas were never there in the first place. In dramatic discourse there is multiple first-second person interplay. The characters speak out in I-Thou relation. The tense orientation is present tense except when characters anticipate the future or recollect the past, in which case future and past tenses come into play. Dramatic discourse is the most vivid of any of the discourse genres. It takes us there in the sense that no other type of discourse takes us. Dramatic discourse is well developed in certain Philippine languages and will be commented on later.

A relatively simple system of paragraph types was evolved for the Philippine structures which were studied. Essentially the paragraph types matched the discourse types with a proviso that, as seen above, we should not necessarily expect a narrative discourse to be composed of narrative paragraphs, nor a procedural discourse of procedural paragraphs. We can expect a certain amount of explanatory and even hortatory material in either genre. Furthermore, expository and hortatory discourse can absorb a limited amount of narrative and procedural material into their broad framework as well.

Narrative and procedural paragraphs have systematic internal devices for linking sentence with sentence. In Philippine structures the typical device is that of a back reference in the onset of one sentence to the previous sentence. The back reference is typically done by the use of a construction which involves a focusless verb, sometimes referred to as the gerundive. It is typically prefixed by *pag-* or *ka-* in Philippine structures. It may be translated 'having done x (we did y)' or in the case of procedural paragraphs 'When you have done x (then do y)'. X is the activity described in the previous sentence. Y is a new activity described in the sentence under examination. Sometimes a back reference is made not by means of a gerundive construction but by means of a subordinate clause much like a 'when' or 'while' clause in English. In some cases, noticeably in Bontoc, the back reference is by virtue of an independent clause whose sole distinguishing feature is the fact that it is a back reference to the previous clause while the succeeding independent clause contains the new information. In some languages, noticeably within the Manobo complex on Mindanao, we find special verb forms called irrealis or dependent verbs which are used in the back reference part of the sentence (as well as in a few other syntactic uses). In some respects this use of dependent versus independent verb is reminiscient of the medial-final verb distinction found in New Guinea highlands languages (Longacre, 1972a).

Needless to say, in the study of a particular Philippine language this device of back reference must be carefully catalogued grammatically, understood, and brought under control for purposes of generation and composition. Within the context of, for instance, the Dibabawon language it is possible to distinguish clearly the type of back reference found in the narrative paragraph from that found in the procedural paragraph. The same two paragraph types may also be distinguished as to consistency of the use of back reference within the paragraph framework. Thus in Bontoc, while almost every two successive sentences of a procedural paragraph are linked by back reference in the succeeding sentence, in a narrative paragraph, although any two successive sentences which display narrative movement may be so linked, it is not considered good style to link more than approximately 50% of them by such an overt device.

Explanatory and hortatory paragraphs do not have linkage by back reference but involve parallelism and a certain amount of mutual cross-reference found in the subordinative parts of the component sentences, e.g., in what I refer to as cause margins and purpose margins. In expository paragraphs there is flow through parallelism, i.e., their essential device is paraphrase with amplification. This is much like the topic sentence plus development of traditional rhetoric. As any good teacher of rhetoric knows, the topic sentence must not be baldly repeated. It is echoed in succeeding sentences and new items of information are deftly worked into the framework. Hortatory paragraphs, as distinct from expository paragraphs, display more of a penchant for use of constructions referring to cause and purpose; i.e., since hortatory discourse sets out to influence conduct, we find many expressions such as "you shouldn't do so and so because..." or "you should do so and so in order to..." There is more tossing back and forth of the content structure between the sentence nucleus and sentence margins of the sort just illustrated than is customary in expository paragraphs.

Opposed to all these is the dialogue paragraph. While it is customary in English to show paragraph indentation with every change of speaker, this is simply an orthographic device. There is an overall unity to the dialogue paragraph which should not be obscured. The linkage between successive sentences in dialogue paragraphs may be expressed by means of quotation formulas of the sort "When Joe had said that, then Mary said this" in which at the onset of the next sentence the "When Joe had said that" is a back reference much like we find in narrative paragraphs. On the other hand, in dramatic dialogue paragraphs where we have no quotation formulas, repartee itself emerges as the basic structure. In repartee what one speaker says calls for what the next speaker says. Content calls up further content, much as in a game, e.g. badminton, in which the 'birdie' is tossed back and forth from person to person.

There are, then, fundamentally three sorts of linkage devices in the various paragraph types which have been mentioned. Narrative and procedural discourses typically are linked by back reference. Expository and hortatory discourses show a flow through parallelism with, as a further linkage device, the flow of content out into cause and purpose margins – especially in hortatory paragraphs. Dialogue paragraphs show linkage by repartee.

This is not the whole story of paragraph types in Philippine languages. For instance under expository paragraphs, various sorts of expository paragraphs were distinguished, e.g., antithetical and coordinate paragraphs. Any and all paragraph types were considered to be simple or complex, i.e., paragraphs were posited which essentially were sequences of smaller closely linked paragraphs.

In the consideration of dialogue we were on new ground. I found former approaches to dialogue in terms of utterance-response pairs to be inadequate. The use of utterance-response pairs such as question-answer, indeed forms the opening phase of the study of dialogue, but some provision must be made for open-ended dialogue in which points are tossed back and forth repeatedly. Beginning, however, with utterance-response pairs, I distinguished question-answer from proposal-response, and from remark-evaluation – and dubbed these pairs 'lexical structure'. For their grammatical structure I assumed that they consisted of a $Speech_1$ and a $Speech_2$ – subsequently called initiating utterance and resolving utterance by Klammer. To allow for open-ended dialogue it was necessary to assume that there were counter-tokens, i.e. counter-question, counter-proposal, and counter-remark, ensuing in every case in unpaired fashion after any question, proposal, or response. These counter-tokens, again dubbed 'lexical structure', were considered to be $Speech_2$'s in the surface structure – since called the continuing utterance by Klammer. These devices plus a $Speech_4$ – in Klammer's terminology, terminating utterance – rounded out the theory of dialogue as far as its initial expression. All this made possible such a dialogue as the following: *Where were you last night?* ($Speech_1$ question). *Why do you ask me?* ($Speech_2$ counter-question). *And why don't you want to tell me?* ($Speech_2$ counter question). *Oh, I just resent people prying into my affairs, that's all* ($Speech_3$ response). *Okay, okay, forget it* ($Speech_4$ acquiescence).

For an initial statement of the theory of dialogue this was fine. The Philippine report went on, however, to allow for more than two speakers in a dialogue and to allow for a dialogue in which the so-called 'lexical structure' and the grammatical structure are out of phase so that, e.g., within the domain of the same sentence a speaker may answer one question and ask another question, such as, *I went downtown but where did you go?*

As we have said the Philippine project offered, in effect, a laboratory for the study of the range and variety of sentence structure within a related family of languages. In respect to sentence structure in general, however, the model that we had obtained during the previous study of Totonac proved valuable in application during the Philippine studies. In the Totonac materials (Reid and others, 1968) we had assumed that a sentence nucleus could be accompanied by what we call sentence margins, e.g. time margin, *while I was there, when you were in the shop*; cause margin, *because I didn't want to*; purpose margin, *in order to do that*; concessive margin, *although he didn't want me to*; conditional margin, *if that's what you want me to do*, etc. In the Totonac materials, this device was resorted to cut down redundancy between sentence types. Thus, while at one time I had posited such units as behavioral-purpose sentences or effect-cause sentences, I now normally cut off the part called purpose and the part called cause and no longer set up special sentence types to cover examples where such (unspecialized) structures were found. Rather I said that, for the most part, any sentence of any sentence type, whatever the distinctions within its nucleus, could have a cause or purpose margin tacked on it. This evidence, which proved useful on the sentence level in Totonac, gave us precisely the elements which were needed for paragraph linkage when we got to the Philippines. There we found that exploitation of the sentence margins (time margin, cause margin, purpose margin etc.) figured largely in linkage between sentence and sentence in the paragraph. What therefore had been created to serve the needs of sentence structure was confirmed as valid by proving its usefulness on another structural level.

What sort of sentence types are found in the discourse structure of Philippine language? Here, again, it is dangerous to generalize. However, much as in English, we find coordinate sentences, i.e. structures in which a conjunction such as *and* joins successive bases with the open-ended potential of an indefinite number of bases. We find antithetical sentences, i.e. structures in which a conjunction such as *but* occurs in the center of a two-base structure. We find alternative sentences with a conjunction such as *or*.

Nevertheless, some qualification is needed here to allow for idiosyncrasies of structure in certain languages. Thus we find that the coordinate sentence is not a universal feature of language. Some languages, for example Batak (from the island of Palawan, data from Rosemary Rodda), have no coordinate sentence, but rather have several sentences of specialized function; there is no one general sentence which serves the variety of purposes served by the English coordinate sentence. We furthermore found that where English has one antithetical sentence type, we would have two or three sentence types in certain Philippine languages. For example, some Philippine languages have a specialized structure for a negative in the first base followed by a positive in the second base. Thus, while *Your horse is black but my horse is white* is one sentence type, *It's not black but white* is a quite different sentence type. In Agta (Mayfield 1972) there is not only an antithetical sentence but an inversion sentence. The inversion sentence employs a word which in other situations is translated 'because', *It is not black because it is white*, but which is obviously used here in a specialized structure with specialized function. A few languages, e.g. Balangao (data from Joanne Shetler), have three sentence types at this point.

Further frequently occurring types can be mentioned. Philippine languages typically have one or more sentence types which are juxtaposed in structure, much like the English sentences *He's magnificent, he's tremendous* or *I went home, I went home to see what was really going on*. Equational sentences, somewhat like the English *It's a fact that John is stupid*, are typically very elaborate and well-formed structures in Philippine languages. There was considerable analytical ambivalence among project participants regarding setting up conditional sentences in Philippine languages. Some analysts set up only conditional margins, others set up conditional sentence types, and some posited both conditional margins and nuclear sentence types of the if-then variety. This is all discussed carefully in Longacre 1968, Vol.II and is not recapitulated here. Contrafactual conditions came in for special considera-tion, however. In Philippine languages such conditions typically are not marked as very distinct in surface structure from other conditions. Nevertheless, many analysts including Elkins (1971) have felt that the mutually dependent character of both parts in a structure such as *if he had only come I would have been happy* and the double talk involved in this mutual dependency, sets this apart as a nuclear sentence pattern. Some correlative sentences are found much like *As Maine goes so goes the nation*, especially in Tausug (data from Seymour Ashley) where a negative correlative sentence occurs such as *The harder I work the less money I earn, The more I study the less I know,* etc. Sentences involving temporal relations characterize almost all the Philippine languages. Typically there is a sequence sentence (often several such sentence types as in Inibaloi; cf. Ballard, Conrad, Longacre, 1971a) and a simultaneous sentence, i.e. a coordinate sentence whose medial *and* means 'at the same time' or 'while'. Quotation sentences are found, both direct and indirect, with considerable elaboration. Thus in Tausug a system of four quotation sentences is posited, with very elaborate use of varied quotation formulas. Indirect question often emerges as a separate sentence type.

An embryonic form of case grammar has been used in the Philippines since the days of the Pike workshop there in the early 1960's. In my work with Myra Lou Barnard on Dibabawon an attempt was made to extend this situational grammar on up through paragraph and discourse structure. The result is embodied in a joint article of the two of us found as part III of Vol. 1 of the Philippine report (Longacre, 1968). In the text volume (Vol. III, which was not reprinted when Vol. I and II were reprinted in the Summer Institute of Linguistics publications) the Dibabawon texts are accompanied by large fold-out diagrams in which an attempt is made to show both the lexical or situational structure and the grammatical structure. Some of these diagrams are in two colors with black and red distinguishing the two partially diverging tree structures. I have since decided that I would prefer to speak of these so-called lexical or situational relationships as notional or deep grammar rather than as lexical structure — which I now reserve for the typical stuff which dictionary makers are concerned with. However, the split-level analysis of Dibabawon text with partially diverging tree graphs remains as a project accomplishment worthy of eventual reexamination and fresh evaluation.

A further word about dramatic discourse is in order. We are accustomed in Western literature to dramatic discourse in which the various dramatis personae are printed in the left hand margin of the page with resultant running identification of who says what. Philippine dramatic discourse is oral. It is as if we had a play by Shakespeare or Oscar Wilde or Sheridan with the left-hand margin wiped out so that we had no way to identify who said what except by what is said. We are all familiar of course with more or less extensive passages in novels in which precisely this occurs. I'm thinking of a chapter (33) in Solzhenitsyn's *First Circle* in which two people are talking to each other. Neither one is identified via quotation formula and one has to read about one third of the way through the chapter before he recognizes who the two are that are talking. Such non-marking of participants is the regular course in consistently dramatic discourse in those Philippine languages where this discourse genre is found, noticeable in the Manobo languages. Not all dramatic discourses, however, are 'pure' in this respect; some involve a limited use of participant identification through quotation formula.

The circumstances under which the first such dramatic discourse came to my attention are instructive. Shirley Abbot and I were going over her corpus of text material. She drug out rather apologetically, from the bottom of the stack, a discourse which she said she could not make head or tail of and which seemed to be incoherent. This proved on examination to be a dramatic discourse which describes a wild-pig hunt. The initial impression of confusion was simply a feature of the innate artistry of the text. Speakers were often not identified because it was not necessary for the purpose of the discourse that all speakers be identified. The milieu of a wild-pig hunt is described by letting everyone speak out in his own right. In some of the component dialogue paragraphs of this discourse one does not know whether two people speak or maybe four. Furthermore, this consideration is not relevant for the purposes of this discourse. On the other hand, the discourse does involve a limited use of quotation formulas in discourse-initial position, in discourse-final position and at the denouement of the discourse (where the pigs are killed). What is interesting here is that what the analyst, from the standpoint of his own background and culture, is likely to reject as a poorly formed text emerges as exemplary of a favorite discourse type of the language community. They, the speakers of the language, find such discourses very congenial, so much so that dramatic discourse is excellent for use in early literacy material to encourage people to read with interest and appreciation.

Besides my own summary (Longacre, 1968) of the results of the Philippine workshop program, some of the subject data of the project has been published in its own right. The excellent monograph by Lawrence A. Reid on Bontoc (1970) contains, among other things, one of the most careful descriptions of sentence structure ever written within the tagmemic framework. A great amount of detail is compactly summarized for each sentence type and the resulting system – in three dimensions – is of interest in itself. A careful set of rules is given to distinguish phonological from grammatical sentences. Of considerable interest as well, is Reid's treatment of procedural discourse. A body of analyzed text is appended to the volume.

A second monograph (1971), in memory of Betty McLachlin (a workshop participant who died in an automobile accident soon after the conclusion of the workshop's program) contains contributions by McLachlin and Blackburn (Sarangani discourse and paragraph), Wrigglesworth (Discourse and paragraph in Ilianen Manobo), Whittle (Discourse and paragraph in Atta), and Walton (Paragraph structure in Binongan Itneg). These articles are built on essentially the same model of analysis and probably show well both the strength of the model and its weaknesses. The McLachlin and Blackburn article, as well as that by Hazel Wrigglesworth, is especially rich in attention to conjunctions and their role in Philippine paragraph and discourse structures. The Whittle article is in some ways the most original and deviant. Walton's article contains some especially interesting examples of one-paragraph procedural discourses involving alternative and simultaneous structures. Analyzed corpora of text occur with the various languages.

In addition, three sentence systems have been published so far, Elkin's Western Bukidon Manobo (1971), Roy Mayfield's Agta (1972) and Hall's Siocon Subanon. Articles on Mansaka sentence and paragraph are in press in a Mansaka monograph (to appear in the Summer Institute of Linguistics Publications in Linguistics). Other excellent articles on sentence structure await editing in the files of the Philippine Branch.

The New Guinea workshop program (OE 0-097756-4409(014)) got going approximately one-and-a-half years after the close of the Philippine workshops. The big concern in the early months of the New Guinea workshop was how to account hierarchically for the phenomenon of clause chaining. Where would we find such old familiar units as sentence and paragraph in languages of this sort — and indeed should we find them at all?

Clause chaining, as a surface structure phenomenon, had been well in hand since the days of a workshop by Pike approximately a decade earlier. It has been recognized since then that the following situation held: 1) Medial clauses with medial verbs occur in an indefinite chain until the final link is reached which is a final clause with a final verb. Such a chain can be extensive — 100 clauses or more, although the size to which chains are built depends on the particular language under consideration. 2) The final verb (sometimes called independ verb) is a verb of peculiar structure found only once in a chain and characteristically at its end. (This picture is somewhat over-simplified in that in some languages there is a distinction of independent and dependent, as well as of medial and final, which crisscross each other, thus giving four resultant verb types.) The final verb is fully marked for tense and mood while medial verbs often are not so marked. 3) Medial verbs, furthermore, have certain features not found in final verbs, namely a preoccupation with the question as to whether the following clause has the same or different subject than itself. In some languages, special suffixes exist to mark same versus different subject relative to that of the following clause. In others this function is marked in portmanteau morphs which indicate still other functions as well (e.g. tense and aspect). Furthermore, some languages not only mark same versus different subject, but add to medial verbs an affix which tells what the subject of the next verb will be, so that a medial verb will have two subject affixes, one indicating its own subject and the other indicating subject of the following verb. 4) Besides this preoccupation with indication of same versus different subject, chaining structures of this sort are also preoccupied with temporal relations. Typically the distinction is between succession, i.e. successive events, and overlapping, i.e. partially or completely simultaneous events. 5) These two concerns, preoccupation with marking of the same versus different subjects, and preoccupation with the marking of various sorts of temporal relations, crisscross in all sorts of idiosyncratic ways from language to language, making an almost unbelievable variety of surface structures even within a fairly compact geographical area. Some languages have structures exclusively of the chaining variety. Others have at least some structures which allow two independent verbs in the same sentence and thereby mix nonchaining with chaining structures. Still others, such as Daga, have almost no clause chaining and what does occur is restricted in a very peculiar fashion (e.g. limited to certain persons and tenses).

The question was therefore very insistent at the onset of the New Guinea project as to what to make of such chains hierarchically. Should we look for our old friends sentence and paragraph in such structures or had we better forget them entirely? The first break came in the study of Foré with Graham Scott. Here it appeared that we had not one kind of medial verb, but two kinds of medial verbs. Medial verbs which marked simultaneity (overlapping) versus sequence (succession), and indicated the same subject in the following clause, seemed to figure in one sort of chain. A different and more inclusive sort of chain could end in a medial verb which indicated different subject in the following clause, but which could not be marked for simultaneity versus succession. Either sort of medial verb was incomplete in itself until followed by a final independent verb. There appeared to be two thresholds in such structures: 1) same subject chains of medial verbs which terminate with different-subject medial verbs and which mark internal relations of simultaneity versus succession. 2) different subject chains of different-subject medial verbs — any of which could terminate a chain of type (1) — but with a final verb at the end of the whole. In terms of the size units involved it seemed plausible to call the same-subject chain a sentence, and the chain which ends with an independent verb and which can mark different-subject relationships within it, the paragraph. This proved insightful for the analysis of discourse in Foré. As evidential of this I cite the published monograph of Graham Scott, "Higher levels in Foré grammar" (1973) and ask the reader to turn to the discourse level trees which occur after the various analyzed discourses. Here there is a plausible structure in terms of same-subject chains (sentences) which build into different-subject chains (paragraphs) which in turn build into discourses.

Discourses of various genres are embraced in Scott's corpus. There are noticeable differences in the length of sentence and paragraph from genre to genre. All this is seen on even a cursory inspection of Scott's discourse-level trees which follow each analyzed text. An interesting sidelight here is that in general, descriptive, expository, and hortatory discourse have a much simpler sentence and paragraph structure than has narrative discourse. This is quite the converse of Western European structure where expository discourse is typically much more involved than narrative style. In terms of the translation of such a document as the Greek New Testament into a language such as Foré, we find that where the Greek New Testament has short sentences (e.g. in the narrative portions of the Gospels), a language such as Foré must have long sentences, and where the Greek New Testament has long involved sentences (noticeably in Romans and other Pauline Epistles) a language such as Foré must have short sentences.

Foré was instructive as an example of a language exclusively of the chaining variety. A few other such languages are Kosena, Kanite, and Telefol.

From this emerges a very different picture of sentence structure from that which we find in the Philippines, in English and other Indo-European languages, and in Mesoamerica. In brief, Highland New Guinea exemplifies choo-choo train structures while the Philippines, English, and Mesoamerica exemplify flight formation structures. In choo-choo train structures, there is an indefinite number of cars (medial clauses with medial verbs) which are hooked to one engine (the final clause with its final verb). In flight formation languages there may be several clauses of equal rank (independent or coordinated clauses). Thus, while in English it is possible to say, *I went downtown but Mary stayed home*, in a choo-choo train language one must choose one of these verbs for special treatment and downgrade the other verb to a medial verb. Thus we'd have *I went downtown* with *went* expressed as a medial verb, *but Mary stayed home* with *stayed* expressed as a final verb. A conjunction or an affix of some sort on the first verb would serve to indicate the *but* or adversative function. This all seemed very novel at the time that we were working through it in the New Guinea materials. I've since had cause to believe that choo-choo train languages are found not solely in New Guinea but in South America and in certain Indian languages of the continental United States, such as Pomo of California (data from Judith Ravenhill), and Crow (data from Ray Gordon). These two types of sentence structures may in fact represent two ways of building sentences the world over. All the sentences of a language may be of one sort or the other, or the two sorts of structures may occur side by side within the same language.

A further thing that emerges from the study of New Guinea structures is that, as we have long suspected, sentence is not necessarily as independent as we have been led to believe since the days of Bloomfield, whose definition of sentence has been vigorously criticised by both Pike and Waterhouse. In fact, in New Guinea chaining languages of the sort exemplified in Foré, the sentence is clearly a dependent unit; it is a subchain within a larger chain. Furthermore, we find within such languages grammatical closure on the paragraph level, closure of the sort that we are not accustomed to finding in Indo-European languages. It is as if the customary sort of things which we find marking the end of a sentence, have moved on up to close the end of the paragraph, and other kinds of markers have evolved to mark sentences within the bigger chain.

Such languages make an ideal laboratory situation for studying encoding of the same surface structure in sentence versus paragraph. We all know that even in English it is possible to build a sentence of paragraph length or to build a paragraph which scarcely exceeds the size of a run-of-the-mill long sentence. It is evident that sentence and paragraph differ in internal organization not in size per se. In Wojokeso (West 1973), the medial final chain is the domain of the sentence, not the domain of the paragraph, so that grammatical closure is found on the sentence, not on the paragraph. Here, however – in spite of the lack of grammatical closure on the paragraph – we still have a situation quite unparallel to English or anything Indo-European, where the sentence does not have morphologically marked grammatical closure such as we find in New Guinea. In Wojokeso we know in a very straightforward manner when we have a sequence of sentences (i.e. a paragraph) versus but one sentence of paragraph length. Consequently, in Wojokeso as compared to English, we have a better set-up for the study of the relative functional load of structures on the two hierarchical levels.

In this regard West mentions that a procedural paragraph may consist of a series of steps, each step being a slot filled by an individual sentence, or it may be a long one-sentence paragraph in which all the steps are given in the same surface-structure sentence. What is the rationale of such a choice? When does one know when to use a series of sentences to encode procedure and when to use one long run-on sentence? We find also the same distinction in narrative paragraphs. The successive events of a narrative paragraph may be given as a series of what I call build-ups, each in a separate sentence, or the whole narrative action may be expressed in one long run-on sentence with but one final verb at its end, i.e. in a one-sentence paragraph. What is the rationale of this choice? Is this pure caprice?

At this point the study of whole discourses is helpful. In fact, a perusal of the Wojokeso corpus of text material (Longacre 1972a, Text) suggests a resolution of the problem. There is a narrative discourse which has narrative paragraphs composed of fair-to-middling-length sentences until one reaches what is really the *denouement* of the whole story. At this point, we find a long run-on structure in which all the events are lumped together in one paragraph-length sentence. Similarly, we have a procedural discourse on housebuilding, in which likewise we find sentences of fair-to-middling length until we reach the *target procedure* where the house is finished and the couple move in to spend their first night in it. Here again we find a long run-on one-sentence paragraph in which all the steps of the paragraph are in one page-length sentence. Sentence is here being used in both narrative and procedural discourse to mark the *peak* of the discourse in the surface structure, which corresponds to either denouement in narrative discourse, or to target procedure in procedural discourse.

Parallels are not lacking elsewhere. Thus, Charles Green has pointed out to me that a not dissimilar phenomenon is found in Hemingway's story, "The short happy life of Francis Macomber". Here at the climax of the story where the main character of the story is shot in the back of the head (accidentally ?) by his wife, we find a long run-on, rollicking sentence not unlike in kind from what we have mentioned in the Wojokeso discourses. Something similar is found in the text of the Greek New Testament. We find in the account of the feeding of the five thousand (Matthew 14: 13-21) an absolutely unparalleled string of participles in sentence initial position. Again this is reminiscent of the run-on style of such a New Guinea language as Wojokeso. Furthermore, we find this string of participles in sentence-initial position precisely at the denouement of the account (Matthew 14:19), where Jesus takes the loaves, multiplies them, and feeds people.

New Guinea with its morphologically marked closure either on sentence or paragraph or both, encourages us to believe in the reality of both sentence and paragraph and in the vitality of their function in discourse. I have, for example, been encouraged by my study of New Guinea materials to apply myself to the analysis of sentence and paragraph within the Greek New Testament — a project in which I am currently engaged.

A further way in which the New Guinea project differed from the Philippine project was the preoccupation with the question of deep versus surface structure in New Guinea languages. This, however, was essentially an outgrowth of the Philippine project. My colleague, Lee Ballard, had written a paper about Inibaloi sentences which did not suit me. It was highly aberrant from the other papers. It became evident that the source of this aberrancy was Ballard's interest in the semantic, underlying, or notional structures — which he had let considerably skew and obscure his presentation of the surface structures in Inibaloi. The answer to our questions seemed to lie in the direction of disentangling the two sorts of structure. Consequently, Ballard joined the New Guinea workshop for one month during which his materials were rewritten from this split-level point of view. At this juncture, I ceased talking about lexical (or situational) versus grammatical structures as I had in the Philippines and began to talk about deep and surface grammar. It seemed to me desirable to keep these two structures within the same hierarchy so that I could range in relative depth, as superficially or as deeply as I cared to carry the analysis. Otherwise, if we had surface structure in one hierarchy and notional structure in a different hierarchy, we would forever be occupied with questions of how to split the pie. Furthermore, we would be left with a dichotomy where what I wanted was a polar opposition with varying degrees of depth between the two poles.

The result was a series of two articles with three authors, Ballard, Conrad, Longacre (1971a, 1971b) in which Ballard was responsible for the structure of Inibaloi, Robert Conrad was responsible for the adaptation of the logical symbolism employed, and I was responsible for the general orientation. What we did in effect was to take the statement calculus of formal logic and enrich and vary it enough to make it adequate for the description of a natural language. In much the same way, Fillmore had previously taken the predicate calculus of formal logic and enriched and varied it for the purposes of linguistic analysis in what became known as case grammar.

The three of us hoped that the enriched and enlarged statement calculus would be a universal apparatus. This apparatus underwent preliminary testing in various languages within the scope of the New Guinea project, is still being tested and modified, and has already gone through several revisions. The most recent revision of the apparatus is in a current volume of mine, *An anatomy of speech notions.* But a former version of the same apparatus is found not only in the series of two articles by Ballard, Conrad, and Longacre, but in chapter three of the New Guinea report itself (Longacre 1972a). Fundamentally the same apparatus (give and take a few categories and change a few labels) has been evolved independently by John Beekman (1970, 1974).

In processing the New Guinea materials, I had an ambitious manual filing project in which I set out to handle sentence structures in a variety of New Guinea languages filed as to both deep and surface structures. My manual file, which I made then and still have, includes data from eight languages. It reaches about the extreme limit of manual filing. I found that in writing up the data for the New Guinea report, I could not as a matter of fact process and generalize from all eight languages, because of the sheer bulkiness of the results. I therefore restricted my attention to three languages and tried to describe the deep and surface structure of both sentence and paragraph in these three: Wojokeso, data from West and now published as a monograph in its own right (1973); Kosena, data from Doreen Marks, now being prepared for publication; and Daga, data from Elizabeth Murane, now edited and incorporated in a large monograph published by the Summer Institute of Linguistics (1974).

In the study of these three languages, I was concerned with the relative distribution of functional load between sentence and paragraph; the relative elasticity (to be defined later) of one sentence type or paragraph type against other units on the same level; and the comparison of the three languages with each other. Wojokeso has the simplest sentence structure and the most involved paragraph structure. Kosena has involved sentence and paragraph structure, as does Daga. Wojokeso marks the sentence grammatically but not the paragraph. Kosena marks both the sentence and paragraph grammatically. Daga customarily marks neither one very clearly but is more like English or some other Indo-European language in this regard.

In Wojokeso many things customarily expressed in the English sentence can be expressed only as a paragraph, i.e. as a sequence of two or more sentences. Among these are various kinds of antithesis and alternation — which are expressed very easily as *but* sentences and *or* sentences in English. Comparison is likewise expressed in Wojokeso only as a paragraph structure. Thus where English can say *The white man's boats are bigger than the black man's boats*, Wojokeso must say something on this order: *The white man's boats are enormous. The black man's boats are small*. In that this is really a variety of contrast, it can be argued that comparison as a category does not really exist in this language.

By relative elasticity of surface structure I meant and mean the following: Over how many deep structures may a given surface structure stretch? How versatile is it? We find for example in English that the coordinate sentence is very versatile, i.e. very elastic, while we find that by contrast an English reason sentence with medial *for* or a result sentence with medial *so* is much less elastic.

I also spoke some in the same volume of relative transparency of surface structures. By this I mean, to what degree is a surface structure marked? If a surface structure is well marked it is considered to be opaque and may easily be thrown out of phase with the underlying structure. If on the other hand a surface structure is poorly marked we may say, so to speak, that the deep structure shines through it. At times we are uncertain of our surface-structure analysis and perhaps go more by the underlying structure. I believe that these two concepts, relative elasticity and transparency of surface structures, could figure in the development of a theory of surface structure.

In other respects the New Guinea workshop was a continuation of the Philippine workshop. Discourse genres were posited much as in the Philippines, although Alan Healey was constantly prodding us to broaden our perspective and look at other sorts of discourse such as he was suggesting. We trust that Healey himself will publish in this regard. As to paragraph types, where we had a relatively simple system with few types in the Philippines, we characteristically obtained very complex systems with many types in New Guinea. Partially this reflects the fact that in certain New Guinea languages there is a greater functional load on the paragraph as opposed to the sentence level. Partially also it reflects the fact that distinctions tend to grow and be elaborated as a taxonomy matures. I sometimes facetiously speak in this regard of the 'budding system' versus the 'blooming' system.

One very important contribution of the New Guinea workshop is an unpublished paper of Alan Healey's called "Are there grammatical paragraphs in English? " In this paper Healey does for English essentially what we did in the various New Guinea languages in the course of the project. He bases his work on a fairly extensive corpus involving travelogue materials, portions from the writings of J.R.R. Tolkien, and some medical writings. So the corpus is considerably varied. He bases his theory of English paragraph structure almost entirely on the rich system of sequence signals and conjunctions found in English. In this respect English contrasts with the average Philippine language, even with such a language as Ilianen Manobo (Wrigglesworth 1971) or Sarangani Bilaan (McLachlin and Blackburn 1971) where there are enough conjunctions to provoke sections of respectable length (in the articles cited) on the role of conjunction in intraparagraph linkage. Nevertheless, even in such languages as these, we find a paucity of conjunctions and sequence signals as compared to English which fairly runs riot in elaborating signals of this sort. Healey has, therefore, concentrated exclusively on these signals and has not considered the use of *back reference* in English. I personally believe that a balanced view of English paragraphs must consider not only the conjunctions of English but the type of linkage obtained through back reference. I have made a step in the direction of showing what I mean in the opening sections of Longacre 1970c.

From the workshop experiences in the Philippines and New Guinea, plus a certain amount of work done on discourse in Mexican Indian languages, I became anxious to make a broader synthesis. Specifically, I wanted to know more about the structure of discourse in English itself. This drove me to the consideration of novels and short stories by English and American authors. The result is embodied in a paper which grew out of my teaching at the L.S.A. Linguistic Institute 1971 (State University of New York at Buffalo): "Narrative versus other discourse genre" (1972b). In this article I accept the classical rhetorician's scheme of drama and climatic narrative as the deep structure of discourse. That is, I assume that discourse has exposition, inciting moment, mounting tension, climax, denouement, final suspense, and closure. I paraphrase this as 'lay it out', 'get something going', 'keep the heat on', 'knot it up proper', 'begin loosening it', 'continue loosening it', and 'wrap it up'. I then raise the question as to how the surface structure of narrative relates to all this. In surface structure we often find that there are clearly marked ways of indicating the exposition in a surface-structure discourse-level tagmeme which we can call stage, and a way of bringing the curtain down in a discourse-level tagmeme which we can call closure. I consider, however, that aperture ('One upon a time...') and finish ('That's all') within the surface level have no deep-structure counterparts but are mechanical and formulaic ways of opening and closing a discourse. We may also find in the surface structure of some discourses a clearly marked peak. The recognition of the peak is important because we can now articulate a considerable amount of the surface structure of a discourse relative to its peak. We can speak for example of pre-peak episodes and post-peak episodes. The peak itself will correspond to either the climax or the denouement in the underlying structure. A discourse may in fact mark two surface-structure peaks in which the first peak corresponds to the deep-structure climax and the second peak corresponds to the deep-structure denouement. This is discussed at length and exemplified in the article mentioned. The surface-structure peak is marked in a variety of ways including such devices as the crowded stage, rhetorical underlining (i.e. use of paraphrase and amplification at a crucial point of the story), and changes of pace in respect to tense, person, viewpoint, length of constituent units (compare the Wojokeso one-sentence paragraphs in narrative and procedural discourse), and use of such things as rhetorical question, shift from non-dialogue to dialogue, or from dialogue to drama. I sensed after writing this article that the surface-structure peak is by no means limited to the structure of narrative and procedural discourses but that other types of discourse (as I should have known) also have peaks which are marked in various ways in them as well. Thus, it is not uncommon in expository and hortatory discourse to use rhetorical underlining to mark the peak.

This brings me up to the present time as far as my own work in the structure of discourse. I'm at present further elaborating the deep and surface structure of discourse especially in respect to genre classification.

6. It is now high time to get back to the consideration of the contribution of other tagmemicist to the study of discourse. Here the contributions of Wise and Klammer are outstanding. Wise's dissertation (1968) has had considerable influence. While it was a study of discourse in Nomatsiguenga (Peru) it especially angled in on the matter of identification of participants. The volume starts out with an example from Nomatsiguenga which underlines the difficulty of identifying participants in translation gloss because of the great difference in participant identification devices in Nomatsiguenga as opposed to English. Indeed, the literal translation of the Nomatsiguenga is incomprehensible. We don't know who did what to whom. Wise then lauches into a discussion of the matter of form versus meaning, and the mutual relationships of the two in discourse. She posits three aspects of meaning: Observer viewpoint, plot of the events narrated, and social setting; and three aspects of form: lexemic, grammatical, and phonological. The intersection of the two gives enough grist for her mills to grind out a volume.

Wise then proceeds to discuss participant identification in the grammatical hierarchy on the levels of clause, phrase, sentence, and paragraph. Thus she is not only able to run in a description of structures on these various levels but to integrate them in every case into the structure of discourse. After that she turns to the description of what she calls L-clauses, i.e. lexical clauses, as well as L-phrases, L-sentences, and L-paragraphs. She also runs in a further unit, the L-chapter, which she feels is important to the description of discourse. I am critical of her work here and there in certain sections in that it seems to me that certain things called lexical are so well marked in the surface structure that they might well have been called grammatical constructions even from her own point of view. In general, I would like to see her grammatical constructions somewhat enriched at the expense of certain things which she now allocates to the lexical constructions. But this is a rather small criticism compared with the outstanding contribution of the work as a whole. In the fifth chapter of her dissertation she brings together lexical and grammatical considerations and brings them to bear on identification of participants in specific discourses. Chapter six stirs in phonological considerations and considers general problems which have to do with aspects of form and aspects of meaning.

A fascinating section (203ff.) of Wise's monograph has to do with informant reaction in relation to paragraph boundaries. She reported that, for the most part her dissection of the text material into paragraphs agreed with the informant's own dissection. Here and there, there was divergence of her dissection from the informant's. While she was tempted to attribute some of this to the informant's lack of attention, she says: "there is yet another explanation which strikes me as being more plausible: in some cases the boundaries of units in L-chapters were more obvious to him than the boundaries of G-paragraphs." (204). She says further on (205), however: "in general, however, he placed boundaries between grammatical rather than lexemic structures. A review of the paragraph boundaries indicated by the informant in other discourses as well as in these two shows that there is a high degree of correlation with the grammatical paragraphs I have posited on formal grounds."

Klammer's dissertation (1971) 'The structure of dialogue paragraphs in written dramatic and narrative discourse' is an exhaustive application and testing of my modest scheme of dialogue structure sketched in a few pages of the Philippine report. One very obvious improvement which Klammer makes is terminological, i.e. he replaced my $speech_1$, $speech_2$, $speech_3$, and $speech_4$, by initiating utterance, continuing utterance, resolving utterance, and terminating utterance, respectively. More than that, Klammer posited a useful distinction between narrative dialogue paragraphs and dramatic dialogue paragraphs. Narrative dialogue paragraphs are typically found in narrative discourse and have quotation formulas introducing the utterances of the various speakers. Dramatic dialogue paragraphs are most typically found in drama and do not have quotation formulas introducing the utterances of the various speakers. Klammer also made some changes in the direction of making more room for nonverbal behavior than I had allowed in my own framework. He espouses the Pike-Wise division into grammar and lexicon rather than my present division into surface and deep grammar. This reflects, however, a change on my part subsequent to the Philippine materials which Klammer had seen – although I would hazard the guess that had Klammer seen my present materials he would still have preferred to have stayed within the Pike-Wise framework since his basic orientation lies in that direction. Klammer has a peculiar use of syntagmeme which I do not find congenial, i.e. he considers a syntagmeme to be the conflated structure in three hierarchies. I would rather say that a syntagmeme is *either* grammatical or phonological – and hold open the possibility of positing lexical syntagmemes of an irregular sort as in idiom formation. But these differences are small compared to the fact that Klammer has given the theory of dialogue structure which I posited very adequate and thorough testing in two extensive and unrestricted corpora, viz. Dickens' novel, *Great Expectations*, and Shakespeare's play *I Henry IV*. He has shown that my germinal scheme is capable of very serious and detailed development and application.

7. It remains to mention the massive contribution of Pike, Trail, and Hale to the understanding of discourse in the recent Nepal-India workshops program in which they have engaged. Unfortunately this extensive material (Trail 1973, in four volumes; Hale 1973a, in four volumes) comes to me too late for me to study it in detail before I must complete the present chapter. I therefore will have to content myself with a brief summary based on not as careful a reading of the materials as I would like to make.

Trail devotes considerable space to the discussion of the sentence as a linguistic unit within discourse. He takes issue with my distinction of sentence versus clause as hierarchical levels but in the end settles for the distinction as a practical convenience. He then works out in detail a taxanomy of deep structure appropriate to the sentence under the rubric "Semantic relations between whole propositions in English" (1973.1. 5-34). This taxonomy can be fruitfully compared with the catalogue of 'the deep structure of interclausal relations' which Ballard, Conrad, and myself (1971a, 1971b) worked out and with Beekman's 'relation between propositions' (1970, 1974).

Following Stall (1961), Trail ranks logical connections according to relative strength of cohesion, with biconditionality outranking conditionality

38

which in turn outranks conjunction and disjunction. In the process he quotes a sentence example from me (Longacre, 1968.2.6):

> *"Because water is scarce some take sponge baths but others have stopped bathing entirely."*

Trail assumes here that 1) cause-effect (implication) outranks antithesis (conjunction); and therefore 2) this sentence should be called a 'Reason-Result sentence'. He explicitly rejects my analysis into cause margin plus sentence nucleus which is here antithetical. Trail has here, I believe, confused grammatical and logical relations. The grammatical distinction of sentence margin versus nucleus (as I conceive it) does not necessarily correlate with logical relations of dominance as Trail (following Stoll) conceives them. It seems to me that the grammatically dominant part of the sentence can be logically less important while the grammatically marginal part of the sentence can be logically dominant. As to the margin-nucleus distinction itself it is rooted in a tradition (now old in English grammar) that *and, but,* and *or* are coordinates and join independent or 'main' clauses while words such as *because, in order to, when,* and *while* serve to attach subordinate clauses. Furthermore, the usefulness of sentence margins such as I posit for the explanation of cohesion within the paragraph, argues for their validity as linguistic units.

Trail believes that the surface structure of the sentence includes only the distinction *coordinate* versus *subordinate* with the former divided into linked versus paratactic structures, and with the latter divided 'between those structures whose dependent half is participial in form and those whose dependent half is made so by the presence of a relator' (28). Sentence types as Trail and those following him envision are apparently reached by a joint consideration of surface structure grammar (as defined above) with semantic considerations — with the latter apparently the most useful (since they include many more distinctions). Thus, in regard to Kupia, R.B. and J.E. Christmas write: "To be contrastive, ordinarily two sentences must have at least one grammatical *and* one semantic difference. We reserve the right, however, to set up sentences (as types) which appear to be contrastive, but for which insufficient evidence is presently at hand" (Trail 1973.1. 133).

Hale (a transformational-generative grammarian with recent interest in tagmemics) is able to tie the work on sentence structure in his volume more closely into the structure of discourse. His introductory chapter "Toward the systematization of display grammar" (Hale 1973b.1. 1-37) contains a brief but significant section: 'Discourse: approaches to the structure of speech acts.' (21-32). In three paragraphs (31-32) which conclude this chapter, Hale raises the question of 'sentence patterns and where they fit.' To me, this seems to be one of the central problems of discourse grammar – only I would generalize the question to one concerning lower-level structures in general and their place in discourse. Specifically, however, Hale mentions the role of subordinate clauses in discourse structure: 1) in the identifying of a paragraph type by means of 'the initial subordinate clause of the paragraph' and 2) in what he calls chaining but which I term back-reference (*He came home. Having come home he...*). In regard to the latter he reports that presence or absence of 'chaining' and type of chaining can be crucial to the establishment of discourse genre or in Hale's words the 'identity of the speech act'.

All this is based on the structure of Sunwar (Nepal) which is reported in two articles within the Hale volume: "Chaining and spotlighting: two types of paragraph boundaries in Sunwar" by Schulze and Bieri (Hale, 1973a.1. 389-400) and "an approach to discourse in Sunwar" by Bieri and Schulze (Hale 1973a.1. 401-62). These articles, if I may say so, look to me like pure gold to the student of discourse. They show, furthermore, the influence of Grimes – whose work I have excluded from my summary on the grounds that he is not a tagmemicist and hence not within the scope of this sketch. All of which goes to show the rather inane nature of our sectarian distinctions. Tagmemicists occasionally build on Grimes, and Grimes occasionally takes a cue or two from the rest of us – and so progress continues.

Pike's technique of 'paired sentence reversal' for the study of discourse (cf. Pike and Pike, 1972) is illustrated in two articles in these volumes, one by Pike and Schöttelndreyer (Hale, 1973a.1. 361-76) on Sherpa (Nepal), and another by Gordon and Pike (Trail 1973.1. 313-43) on Shangar-Kudux (Nepal). The beauty of the technique is that it is an experimental approach to discourse. It enables us to operate on a discourse and evaluate the results of the operation. The operation is simple: pairs of sentences in the text (or larger sections) are reversed and whatever adjustments must be made to preserve intelligibility and well-formedness are made (with the cooperation of native speakers). The results are evaluated. Why were certain reversals easy to make, others difficult, and still others impossible? Surely this cannot fail to tell us something about the structure of connected discourse and cohesion within it. For example, paragraph boundaries (as intuited) are found as places of great difficulty (or impossibility) in regard to sentence reversal across the boundary between two paragraphs.

8. As this article is written, work on discourse continues at unslackened pace on the part of those who call themselves tagmemicists – or at least profess some interest in the approach. Enough preliminary work has already been done to enable us to concentrate on questions such as the following which

should (and probably will) call for considerable attention in the future: 1) How adequate for the study of discourse are the various partial or pretending-to-be-complete cataloque of deep structure notions which Hale, Trail, Beekman, and myself have worked out? What further categories need to be posited? Which need to be combined? How could the whole system be organized in some better way? And finally, how universal are these notions? 2) How are the underlying notional categories related to the grammatical surface structure of discourse? This question has many ramifications. Granted, for example, that a given notional category may be expressed in several different ways grammatically, what is it in the structure of discourse that dictates the selection of one surface structure rather than another? This sometimes involves decision as to the hierarchical level of surface structure on which a notional category encodes. We would like to be able to state better the conditions under which a predication emerges as a surface-structure clause and when it is wholly or partially nominalized. We would like also to state better when a complex of predications is encoded as a sentence and when it encodes as a paragraph. 3) These considerations bring us around again to the ever basic questions of *cohesion* and *prominence* in discourse (Halliday's terms). A discourse starts, stops, and keeps going all the way between. What keeps it going? How is discourse *flow* provided for? Furthermore, certain themes or lexical motifs are played up and others are treated as background In every part of a coherent discourse the flow of the whole requires an evaluation of the relative prominence of each component. In addition to all this a discourse may have a formally marked *peak* — as has been described. All this is partially understood but needs to be understood better. 4) Somewhat related to the preceding is the question: How do the larger units of discourse, e.g. the main discourse itself, embedded discourse, and paragraphs, dictate the structure of smaller parts such as word and clause structures? We need to be able to explain better tense and person selection, occurrence of expressions of time and place, and the distribution of verbals such as infinitives and participles.

Some further questions center around the study of discourse in particular languages: 5) What are the characteristics of wellformed discourse in language Q of linguistic area A? 6) To what degree do these characteristics carry over from language to language in that area and in other areas? 7) Finally, what does the study of language Q contribute to the understanding of discourse and of language in general?

REFERENCES

Ballard, D. Lee, Robert J. Conrad, and R.E. Longacre
1971a   "The deep and surface grammar of interclausal relations", *Foundations of Language* 7, 70-118
1971b   *More on the deep and surface grammar of inter-clausal relations. Language Data*, Asian-Pacific Series, No. 1. Ukarumpa (Papua New Guinea): Summer Institute of Linguistics.
Becker, Alton L.
1965   "A tagmemic approach to paragraph analysis", *College Composition and Communication* 17, 237-42.
1966   "Symposium on the Paragraph", *College Composition and Communication* 17, 67-72.
Beekman, John
1970   "Propositions and their relations within a discourse", *Notes on Translation* 37, 6-27. Ixmiquilpan, Hidalgo (Mexico): Instituto Lingüístico de Verano publication.
- - - -   Beekman, John, and John Callow
1974   *Translating the word of God* (Grand Rapids: Zondervan).
Brend, Ruth (Ed.)
1972   *Kenneth L. Pike, Selected writings* (The Hague: Mouton).
Bridgeman, Lorraine
1966   *Oral paragraphs in Kaiwa (Guarani)*. Indiana University dissertation.
Dijk, Teun A. van
1972   *Some aspects of text grammars* (The Hague: Mouton). (See extensive bibliography of further work, pp. 347-48).
Elkins, Richard
1971   "Western Bukidnon Manobo sentence structure", *Lingua* 27, 216-262.
Firbas, Jan
1961   "On the communicative value of the modern English finite verbs", *Brno Studies in English* 3, 79-104.
1964a   "On defining the theme in functional sentence analysis", *Travaux Linguistiques de Prague* 1 (L'école de Prague d'aujourd'hui), 267-280.
1964b   "From comparative word-order studies (Thoughts on V. Mathesius' conception of the word-order system in English compared with that in Czech)", *Brno Studies in English* 4, 111-126.
1966   "Non-thematic subjects in contemporary English". *Travaux Linguistiques de Prague* 2, 239-256.
1967   "It was yesterday that...", *Sbornik prací filosofické fakulty Brněnské University* A15, 142-6.
Firth, John Rupert
1951a   "General linguistics and descriptive grammar", *Transactions of the Philological Society*, 69-87.
1951b   "Modes of meaning", *Essays and Studies* 4, 118-149 (London: The English Associates).
1955   "Structural linguistics", *Transactions of the Philological Society*, 83-102.
Gleason, H.A. Jr.
1968   "Contrastive analysis in discourse structure", *19th Annual Round Table, Georgetown Monograph Series* 21, 39-63.
Gudschinsky, Sarah C.
1968   "Analisis tagmemico de unidades que combinan componentes verbal y no verbal", *Cuadernos de Antropología* (Instituto de Antropología, Universidad Nacional de Litoral Rosario, Argentina), 43-53.

42

Hale, Austin (ed.)

1973a   *Clause, sentence and discourse patterns in selected languages of Nepal*, Vol.
         1, *General Approach*; Vol. 2, *Clause* (co-ed. D Watters); Vol. 3, *Texts*; Vol.
         4, *Word Lists*. Summer Institute of Linguistics Publications in Linguistics
         and Related Fields, No. 40.
1973b   "Towards the systematization of display grammar", in Hale 1973a. 1-38;
         and in Trail 1973, 3-36.

Hall, William C.
1973   "An outline of siocon subanon sentence structure", *Philippine
         Journal of Linguistics* 4. 1-22.

Halliday, M.A.K. and Ruqaiya Hasan
1973   *Cohesion in spoken and written English* (prepublication copy; to appear in
         Longman's English Language Series).

Harris, Zellig
1946   "From morpheme to utterance", *Language* 22, 161-83.
1952   "Discourse analysis", *Language* 28, 1-30.

Hjelmslev, Louis
1953   "Prolegomena to a theory of language", [Translated by F.J. Whitfield from
         the Danish original, 1943]. *Indiana University Publications in Anthro-
         pology and Linguistics,* Memoir 7, *I.J.A.L*

Jakobson, Roman and John Lotz
1952   "Axioms of a versification system exemplified by the Mordvinian
         folksong", *Linguistica* 1, 5-13, Acta Instituti Hungarici Universitatis
         Holmiensis.

Katz, J.J. and J.A. Fodor
1964   "The structure of a semantic theory", *Language* 39, 170-210.

Klammer, Thomas P.
1971   *The structure of dialogue paragraphs in written dramatic and narrative
         discourse* (Ann Arbor, University of Michigan Dissertation).

Lakoff, Robin
1972   "Language in context", *Language* 48, 907-27.

Longacre, Robert E.
1960   "String constituent analysis", *Language* 36, 63-88.
1965   "Some fundamental insights of tagmemics", *Language* 41, 65-76.
1968   *Discourse, paragraph and sentence structure in selected Philippine
         languages*, 3 volumes (Final Report, Contract No. OE-0-8-062838-0391,
         Dept. of HEW). First two volumes republished as *SIL Publications in
         Linguistics* 21 (Santa Ana).
1970a   "Hierarchy in language", *Method and theory in linguistics*, Ed. by Paul
         Garvin, 173-95 (The Hague: Mouton).
1970b   "Paragraph and sentence structure in New Guinea Highlands languages",
         Kivung 3, 150-63.
1970c   "Sentence structure as a statement calculus", *Language* 46, 783-815.
1971   *Philippine discourse and paragraph studies in memory of Betty
         McLachlin. Pacific Linguistic Series* C 22 (Canberra).
1972a   *Hierarchy and universality of discourse constituents in New Guinea
         languages* (Final report Contract No. OE-0-9-097756-4409(014), Dept. of
         HEW). Two Volumes: Discussion, Texts (Washington: Georgetown.
         University Press).
1972b   "Narrative versus other discourse genre", *From soundstream to discourse,*
         Paper from the 1971 Mid-America Linguistics Conference, Ed. by Daniel G.
         Hays and Donald M. Lance, 167-85.

Loos, Eugene
1961   *Capanahua narrative structure, University of Texas Language and Literature Series.*

Loriot, James and Barbara Hollenbach
1970   "Shipibo paragraph structure", *Foundations of Language* 6, 43-66.

Mayfield, R.
1972   "Agta sentence structure", *Linguistics* 85, 21-66.

McLachlin, Betty and Barbara Blackburn
1971   "An outlet of Sarangani Bilaan discourse and paragraph structure", *Philippine Discourse and Paragraph Studies in Memory of Betty McLachlin.* ed by R.E. Longacre, *Pacific Linguistics Series C* 22 (Canberra: The Australian National University), 1-84.

Murane, Elizabeth
1974   *Daga Grammar,* Summer Institute of Linguistic Publications in linguistics and related fields, 43.

Petöfi, Janos S.
1971   "On the comparative structural analysis of different types of 'works of art' ", *Semiotica* 3.4, 365-78.
1972a   "On the syntactico-semantic organization of text structures", *Poetics* 3.
1972b   "Towards a grammatical theory of verbal texts", *Zeitschrift für Literatur-wissenschaft und Linguistik.*

Pickett, Velma B.
1960   *The grammatical hierarchy of Isthmus Zapotec, Language dissertation* 56 (= University of Michigan, PhD Dissertation, 1959).

Pike, Kenneth L.
1943   *Phonetics*: A critical analysis of phonetic theory and a technique for the practical description of sounds, (Ann Arbor University of Michigan Publications, Vol. IV, Language and Literature, XXI).
1945   *The intonation of American English* (Ann arbor University of Michigan Publications, *Linguistics* 1).
1947   *Phonemics: A technique for reducing languages to writing*, (Ann Arbor University of Michigan Publications, *Linguistics* III).
1948   *Tone languages* (Ann arbor University of Michigan Publications, *Linguistics*).
1964a   "Beyond the sentence", *College Composition and Communication* 15, 129-35 [Reprinted in Brend, 1972].
1964b   "Discourse Analysis and Tagmeme Matrices", *Oceanic Linguistics* 3.1, 5-25.
1966   *Tagmemic and matrix linguistics applied to selected African languages,* (Final Contract Report, Contract OE-5-14-065) (Ann Arbor: University of Michigan Center for Research on Language and Language Behavior) [Republished in 1970 as Summer Institite of Linguistics Publications in Linguistics 23 (Santa Ana)].
1967   *Language in relation to a unified theory of the structure of human behavior* (The Hague: Mouton) [earlier published seriatim in three parts, 1954-1960, Summer Institute of Linguistics].

Pike, Kenneth L. and Ivan Lowe
1969   "Pronominal reference in English conversation and discourse – a group theoretical treatment", *Folia Linguistica* 3, 68-106.

Pike, Kenneth L. and Evelyn G. Pike
1972   "Seven Substitution exercises for studying the structure of discourse", *Linguistics* 94, 43-52.

44

Popovich, Harold
1967   "Large grammatical units and the space-time setting in Maxakali", *Atas de simposio sobre a biota Amazonica* 2, 165-69.
Powlison, Paul
1965   "A paragraph analysis of a Yagua folktale", *IJAL* 31, 109-18.
Reid, Aileen, Ruth G. Bishop, Ella M. Button, and Robert E. Longacre
1968   *Tononac: from clause to discourse,* Summer Institute of Linguistics Publications in Linguistics and Related Fields 17.
Reid, Lawrence A.
1970   *Central Bontoc: sentence, paragraph, and discourse,* Summer Institute of Linguistics Publications in Linguistics and Related Fields 27.
Scott, Graham
1973   "Higher levels of Fore grammar", *Pacific Linguistics,* Series B, 23 (Canberra: Australian National University).
Stall, Robert R.
1961   *Set theory and logic* (San Francisco: W. H. Freeman and Co.)
Trail, Ronald L. (Ed.)
1973   *Patterns in clause, sentence and discourse in selected languages of India and Nepal.* Part I, *Sentence and Discourse*; Part II, *Clause*; Part III, *Texts*; Part IV, *Word Lists.* Summer Institute of Linguistics Publications in Linguistics and Related Fields, 41.
Waterhouse, Viola
1962   *The grammatical structure of Oaxaca Chontal, IJAL* 28.2 (Part 2), Publication 19 of the Indiana University Research Center in Anthropology, Folklore, and Linguistics (University of Michigan PhD dissertation 1958).
1963   "Dependent and independent sentences", *IJAL* 29, 45-54.
Walton, Charles
1971   "Binongan Itneg paragraph structure", in Longacre (ed.), 283-366.
West, Dorothy
1973   *Wojokeso sentence, paragraph and discourse analysis, Pacific Linguistic Series C* 28 (Canberra: Australian National University).
Wise, Mary Ruth
1968   *Identification of participants in discourse; a study of form and meaning in Nomatsiguenga.* PhD Dissertation, University of Michigan (= Summer Institute of Linguistics Publications in Linguistics and Related Fields, 28).
Whittle, Claudia
1971   "Atta discourse and paragraph structure", in Longacre (ed.) 194-282).
Wrigglesworth, Hazel
1971   "Discourse and paragraph structure of Illianen Manobo", (in: Longacre (ed.), 85-194.)
Young, Richard E., Alton L. Becker, and Kenneth L. Pike
1970   *Rhetoric: discovery and change,* (New York: Harcourt, Brace, and World).
Young, Richard E. and ALton L. Becker
1964   "The role of lexical and grammatical cues in paragraph recognition", *Studies in Language and Language Behavior,* Center for Research on Language and Language Behavior 1-6 (Ann Arbor: University of Michigan).
1965   "Toward a modern theory of rhetoric: a tagmemic contribution", *Harvard Educational Review* 23, 450-68.

PHONOLOGY

EUNICE V. PIKE
Summer Institute of Linguistics

INTRODUCTION

Tagmemic phonology is useful for providing insights into the phonological structure of language in general as well as insights into the structure of specific languages. First, by viewing language with the concept of units which contrast with other units, which have a range of variability, and which are distributed in a class of units, in sequences, and in a system. Second, by viewing language as having a hierarchy with smaller units distributed into larger units which are distributed into still larger ones. Third, by viewing language from different perspectives: 1) A stream of speech viewed as a sequence of particles, and as somehow static. 2) The same stream of speech viewed as fluid, dynamic, a wave which causes the units to fuse, or to partially fuse, etc. It is this wave characteristic which causes units to have nuclei and margins. 3) Languages viewed as a field structure with symmetry. A unit is seen as part of the whole, and is really understood only when seen in relation to that whole (see K. Pike, 1973).

The basic theory is that of K. Pike (1967), but examples of application of bits of the theory come from many sources. The chapter is a synthesis, bringing together in outline form the applied bits of theory, making it possible to see the theory as a whole with examples. Perhaps the most important part of my contribution is listing with examples: 1) The criteria for determining a structural level in phonology, Section 1. 2) The features with which emic syllables may be contrasted, Section 2.1. 3) The features with which phonological words may be contrasted, Section 3.2.

1. LEVELS OF THE PHONOLOGICAL HIERARCHY

The phonological hierarchy has various levels, and a sequence of units on the same phonological level is a sequence of rhythm waves. A rhythm wave may be a grouping of smaller waves, and the larger wave may be a unit of one level and the smaller waves within it may be units on a lower level.

The number of levels is not the same for all languages. All languages have a phoneme level, however, and most have a syllable level.

Since it may be a problem to determine the number of levels for a given language, I have listed here the criteria for determining them.

A rhythm wave is not always a unit of a phonological level. Specifically, a rhythm wave, or a grouping of smaller rhythm waves, is not a unit of a phonological level unless the entire text of which it is a part can be divided into units of that level with nothing left over. For example, consonant clusters, although rhythmic groupings, are not units of a phonological level because an entire text cannot be divided into consonant clusters only. For the same reason stressed syllables are not a level. An entire text can, in some specific language for example, be completely divided into phonemes, and also completely divided into syllables, and into phonological words. That language, therefore, may have a phoneme level, and a syllable level, and a word level.

Following are listed three criteria for determining that a rhythm wave, or a rhythmic grouping of smaller waves, is a level of the phonological hierarchy. The level is structurally relevant if any one of the criteria occurs.

1) A level is structurally relevant if the rhythm wave of which it is composed is needed as an environment for conditioning units of a lower level, or for conditioning features of that same level. Following are some instances showing that a level was needed.

(a) Allophones or allotones dependent upon a syllable level.
level.
In Central Bontoc (Reid, 1963:25) /i/ is lowered when it occurs in a syllable checked by a consonant.
In Mikasuki the choice of some allotones is dependent upon whether or not the tone occurs in a long or a short syllable. A long syllable contains a long vowel, or ends in a voiced consonant, or /h/ (West, 1962:81, 83).
In Apinayé of Brazil, the nasals /m, n, ñ, ŋ/ and the spirants /v, r, ž/ all have allophones in accordance with their occurrence in syllable-initial position versus syllable-final position (Burgess and Ham, 1968:9-13, 17).

(b) Allophones dependent upon a phonological-word level.
In Manambu of Papua New Guinea, the voiceless bilabial stop has an unaspirated allophone when in word-initial position, an aspirated allophone when in word-final position, and a voiceless fricative when in word-medial position (Allen and Hurd, 1972:37).
In Kewa of Papua New Guinea (Franklin, 1965:84), /a/ [a] in word initial syllables, [a:] in stressed syllables, [ʌ] fluctuating with [a] in wordfinal syllables and [ʌ] elsewhere.

Newman speaks of the word as a structural unit in Bella Coola. One of the reasons he gives for doing so is that allophones of some of the consonants are determined by "word juncture" — that is by distribution in the word (1947:132).

(c) Allophones dependent upon pause-group level. In Apinayé consonants when final in the pause group have a nonphonemic vocalic release conditioned by the preceding vowel (Burgess and Ham, 1968:16).

2) A level is structurally relevant if the rhythm wave of which it is composed has at least two units on that level which contrast with each other. Following are some instances showing that a level was needed.

(a) Units contrasting on syllable level.

In Sangir of the Philippines, there are four contrastive syllable types: CV, CVC, VC, and V (Maryott, 1961:118).

(b) Units contrasting on phonological-word level.

Words contrast by placement of stress in Spanish, and also in Central Bontoc of the Philippines (Reid, 1963:22).

(c) Units contrasting on pause-group level.

In Eastern Popoloca (Kalstrom and E.V. Pike, 1968:28, 29) the normal pause group ends in a short, loud syllable which ends with a glottal stop. Politeness is expressed when the whole pause group is raised in pitch, and the last syllable is long, lenis, and gets softer as it glides even higher in pitch.

3) A level is structurally relevant if the rhythm wave of which it is composed serves as a distributional matrix for smaller units (K. Pike, 1967:419-20). Following are examples.

(a) Phonemes distributed into the syllable.

Moser and Moser (1965) show how the consonants and vowels are distributed into the syllable of Seri (Mexico).

Newman in arguing that a syllable is not a structural unit in Bella Coola points out that there is no significant grouping of phonemes determined by a syllable (1947:133).

(b) Phonemes are distributed into a phonological word.

In at least seven languages of New Guinea, $/r/$ and $/l/$ occur only between vowels in word-medial position (E.V. Pike, 1964:123).

In Western Popoloca (Mexico) the voiced fricatives occur in stressed syllables but not in nonstressed (Williams and E.V. Pike, 1968:380).

(c) Syllables distributed into the phonological word.

In Shiriana of Brazil and Venezuela, VC syllables occur only in the final position of the phonological word (Migliazza and Grimes, 1961:33, called by them "foot"), and CCVC syllables occur only in the initial position of the word.

In Tarahumara of Mexico (Burgess, 1970:51, 54) a syllable-type CCV does not occur following the word nucleus, but it may occur in the word nucleus, or preceding the word nucleus.

2. SYLLABLE LEVEL

The syllable level (K. Pike, 1967:365-92) is almost universal. (For a language without a syllable level, see Newman's description of Bella Coola, 1947:132-33.) In tagmemic phonology the syllable is a rhythm wave with a nucleus which may or may not be preceded and/or followed by a margin. The nucleus is syllabic; the margin is nonsyllabic.

The syllable as a structural unit of tagmemic phonology began to come into focus when it was observed, for example, that an etic syllable was not necessarily an emic syllable (Elson, 1947:13), that a contoid could be a part of the vowel nucleus (Aschmann, 1946:41, see also K. Pike, 1967:387), and that an emic syllable could be divided between nucleus and margin, and that the margin with consonant clusters, and the nucleus with vowel clusters could be devided again into subordinate and principal members (K. Pike and E.V. Pike, 1947). (For a short summary of non-tagmemic views of the syllable, see K. Pike, 1967:410-12.)

Not all etic syllables are necessarily emic syllables. In Sierra Popoloca, Elson (1947:13) considers CV η (two etic syllables) to be one emic syllable because the [η] is never stressed.

The nucleus of an etic syllable is usually a continuant which is separated from pause by a stop (K. Pike, 1947:147). For example, the [s] of spa, the [h] of aph, the [n] of nda. In determining if an etic syllable is also emic, it is helpful to check the nucleus for: 1) its potential for stress placement, 2) its potential for tone placement, 3) its timing in comparison with syllables known to be emic, and 4) its potential as a unit for describing the distribution of phonemes (K. Pike 1947:144-48, 1967:375-77).

In some languages, one etic syllable may be two emic syllables. For example, in San Miguel Mixtec a long vocoid preceded by a consonant (one etic syllable) is two emic syllables (K. Pike, 1967:376).

The etic border between syllables may be indefinite, and a phoneme at the border point may actually be in double function. That is, it may be simultaneously a member both of the first syllable and of the second syllable (K. Pike, 1967:382).

For determining the emic border between syllables, it is helpful to note the consonants or consonant clusters which occur between pause and the first vowel, and to note the consonants or consonants clusters which occur between the last vowel and pause. By analogy with this, the emic division between syllables can frequently be determined as it occurs word medially or utterance medially (K. Pike, 1947:91). For example, in spoken Greek, Romero (1964:76) has emic syllables, the borders of which are determined by analogy with the initial versus the final consonants of an utterance.

2.1. *Contrastive syllables (the feature mode)*

There are various features by which emic syllables may be contrasted, and there are two ways these features can be handled. The emic syllable with its predominant feature may be considered to be a unit as a whole, in which case one emic syllable contrasts with another (K. Pike, 1967:408-09). Or, the predominant features by which the syllables are contrasted may be considered to be emes, in which case length, nasalization, etc., are considered to be suprasegmental phonemes.

Below are listed the more common features by which emic syllables are contrasted.

(1) The placement of the nucleus.

In Sindangan Subanun of the Philippines, Brichoux (1970:71) lists the following contrastive syllables: CV, VC, CCV, CVC.

In Chepang of Nepal, Caughley (1970:144) lists ten syllables which are contrastive by the placement of the nucleus in relation to the consonants.

2) A simple nucleus with one vowel versus a complex nucleus with more than one vowel.

In Huautla Mazatec there are syllables with one, two, or three vowels (K. Pike and E.V. Pike, 1947:83, 84).

In Daga of Papua New Guinea, a syllable nucleus may have one, two, or three vowels. There is a contrast between vowel clusters which are a complex nucleus versus vowel clusters which are a sequence of syllable nuclei (Murane, 1972:22-24).

Minor (1956) discusses the interpretation of sequences of vocoids in Witoto of Peru. (Witoto has clusters of from two to seven diverse vocoids.) Timing is the main factor which he uses to differentiate between a sequence of vowels which make up a complex syllable nucleus versus a sequence of vowels which are also a sequence of syllable nuclei.
nuclei.

For an example in which a sequence of vowels is considered to be a sequence of syllables rather than a complex syllable nucleus, see Huambisa of Peru (Beasley and K. Pike, 1957:6).

3) A simple nucleus versus a nucleus which includes a glottal stop, /h/, or some other consonant.

In Totonac of Mexico (Aschmann, 1946:41; K. Pike, 1967: 387) the glottal stop is treated as part of the nucleus.

In Siona of Ecuador the Wheelers (1962:108-110) list the three contrastive syllable types: CV versus CVV versus CV?.

In Lalana Chinantec of Mexico, the Rensches (1966: 457-57) describe the way a postvocalic /h/ and /?/ affect the whole syllable. They call them "segmental-prosody phonemes".

In Chicahuaxtla Trique, Longacre concludes that vocoids separated by glottal stop or /h/ may be the complex nucleus of one syllable, or they may consist of two syllables. The two sequences are in contrast. He gives five reasons for his conclusion (1952:75). See also Saxton (1963:32).

In Usila Chinantec of Mexico a post-vocalic /g/ [γ] is considered to be part of the syllable nucleus (Skinner, 1962:252-53). See also, Sochiapan Chinantec (Foris, 1973:234). For a more thorough discussion of a post-vocalic phone which is part of the syllable nucleus, see Merrifield on Palantle Chinantec (1963:6, 7) and Rensch on Lalana Chinantec (1966:456, 457).

Quiotepec Chinantec has perhaps the most complicated syllable nuclei (Robbins, 1968:21-40). In addition to tone, there are the contrastive features of nasalization, glottal stop (with both checked nuclei versus interrupted nuclei), length, accent, and extension. Extension is a continuation of the kernel vowel, but it has its own tone pattern, and may or may not have glottal stop, length, and accent.

4) Tone as a contrastive feature of the syllable.

There are many languages which have tone as a contrastive feature of the syllable although only a few are mentioned here. Tone, in the languages referred to, may not have been described in those terms, however. Some of the languages with syllable tone are: Huautla Mazatec (K. Pike and E.V. Pike, 1947), Yatzachi Zapotec (E.V. Pike, 1948), Mazahua (E.V. Pike, 1951), Huichol (Grimes, 1959), Quiotepec Chinantec (Robbins, 1961), Marinahua (E.V. Pike and Scott, 1962), Mikasuki (West, 1962), Palantla Chinantec (Merrifield, 1963), Amuzgo (Bauernschmidt, 1965), Awa (Loving, 1966), Ayutla Mixtec (Pankratz and E.V. Pike, 1967).

5) Long vowel nucleus versus short vowel nucleus.

In addition to the choice of considering length as a suprasegmental phoneme, or as part of a contrastive syllable, there may be a question as to whether the length should be on the phoneme level (long vowels versus short vowels), or on the syllable level (long syllables versus short syllables).

Following are listed some languages with long syllables versus short syllables (some of these have been described as having long vowels versus short vowels): Huastec of Mexico (Larsen and E.V. Pike, 1949:268), Mikasuki of USA (West, 1962:80), Tifal of Papua New Guinea (Steinkraus, 1969:60-61), Mantjiltjara of Australia (Marsh, 1969:137), Chipaya of Bolivia (Olson, 1967:301).

In Halang (Cooper, 1966:95-97) and in Stieng (Haupers, 1969:133) both of Viet Nam, vowel length is considered to be a "prosody of length". That is, a contrastive feature of the syllable.

In Northern Standard Bhojpuri there is a contrast of long versus short vocoids. In his analysis Trammell has extracted a "component of length" (1971:128-30). He lists as syllable types V versus V·, etc. (1971:134).

The following are examples in which a long vocoid is considered to be a sequence of vowels, rather than a vowel plus suprasegmental length.

In Western Popoloca of Mexico a phonetically long vowel is emically a sequence of two or three vowels, not a syllable with the contrastive feature of length. That is because the language has many other vowel clusters, and because there may be a morpheme break between a cluster of identical vowels (Williams and E.V. Pike, 1968:375). Likewise in Huambisa of Peru, due to the numerous clusters of diverse vowels, the phonetically long vowels are considered to be a sequence of two vowels (Beasley and K. Pike, 1957:5). See also Huichol of Mexico (Grimes, 1969:168).

6) Nasalization

In Secoya of Ecuador, Johnson and Peeke list nasalization as emic on the syllable level (1962:82-84).

Trammell abstracts a "component" of nasalization for Northern Standard Bhojpuri of India (1971:128-30), and he lists syllables with nasalized vowels as one of his syllable types (1971:134).

In Tepetotutla Chinantec of Mexico, Westley (1971:160-61) considers nasalization to be a contrastive feature of the syllable. It seems to me, however, that his analysis would have been neater if he had kept both voiced stops and nasal consonants as phonemes. He chose, instead of having nasal consonants /m/, etc., to mark the place in the syllable where the nasalization was initiated — at the consonant versus at the vowel. That is, he considers a syllable initial [m] to be a nasalized /b/. In his analysis this contrasts with a syllable initial [b] /b/.

The nuclei of Palantla Chinantec have the contrast of oral versus light nasalization versus heavy nasalization (Merrifield 1963:5).

Following are examples in which nasalization is contrastive on the phoneme level.

In Sirionó of Bolivia, nasalization is a contrastive feature on the phoneme level, since there are allophones of the voiceless stops and of nasal consonants which are dependent upon a contiguous oral versus a contiguous nasal vowel (Priest, 1968:103-05).

In Mesquital Otomi of Mexico also, nasalization is a constrative feature on the phoneme level since there is contrast of oral versus nasal vowels following nasal consonants (Sinclair and K. Pike, 1948:92).

7) Ballistic articulation versus controlled articulation.

K. Pike (1967:368-69) analyzes American English as having a contrast of syllables with ballastic versus controlled movement. The last syllable of the following words are some of the examples he used to illustrate the contrast: *tinsel* versus *insult*; *effigy* versus *refugee*. I would add: *Johnson* versus *grandson, happily* versus *jubilee, stucco* versus *indigo*.

Concerning Amuzgo of Mexico, Bauernschmidt (1965:471-75) describes ballistic syllables as having a quick, forceful release with a rapid decrescendo, and the controlled syllable as having a smooth sustained release followed by a gradual, controlled decay. There are numerous allotones in accordance with occurrence in the ballistic versus the controlled syllables.

Concerning Dalfa of India, Ray (1967:10) speaks of a contrast between tense and lax syllables, and he says that the tense syllables "have their pitch transition sharply steeped, frequently accompanied by a redundant glottal stop". Perhaps these syllables correspond to what we have called ballistic versus controlled.

Several of the Chinantec languages of Mexico are described as having ballistic versus controlled syllables. For example, Palantla Chinantec (Merrifield, 1963:2,3), and Tepetotutla Chinantec (Westley, 1971:160, 162). Since, however, they are equated with stress, and occur only on stressed syllables, I now consider the ballistic versus controlled articulatory movement for these languages to be a feature on the word level (see Section 3.2).

8) Velarized versus nonvelarized syllables.

Nasr (1964:454) concludes that the best solution for velarization in Arabic is to consider it a "suprasegmental feature". That is, to consider it a contrastive feature of the syllable. To him, and to me that solution seems better than describing velarized consonants which condition the vowels, or describing velarized vowels which condition the consonants.

Solomon and Headley also posit velarization as a suprasegmental phoneme in Modern Spoken Syriac (1973:143-44).

9) Sibilants versus vowels.
 Olson postulates sibilants as nuclei of syllables in Chipaya of Bolivia on the basis of timing, allophones of preceding consonants, juncture, etc. (1967:302).

2.2. *Variants of syllables (the manifestation mode)*

Syllables usually vary in length in accordance with their distribution into the nucleus of a word versus into the margin of a word. That is, they may be phonetically longer, louder, etc., when stressed (K. Pike, 1967:378).
 Concerning Selepet of Papua New Guinea, McElhanon (1970:16, 17) describes the length variants of syllables as conditioned by their place in units of higher levels, and also as conditioned by the number and type of phonemes.
 Concerning Totontepec Mixe of Mexico, Crawford (1963:94) describes breathy and laryngealized variants of syllables conditioned by voice quality differences due to speech styles.
 In Gurung of Nepal, Glover (1969:40,41) considers the syllable to have variants in accordance with the phonemes that fill the various C and V slots. That is my choice also, but K. Pike (1967:373) described syllables containing different phonemes as being contrastive syllables.

2.3. *Distribution of syllables*

Syllables are distributed into higher levels of the phonological hierarchy, and in some languages there are restrictions as to which contrastive syllables may occur in the different slots of the larger phonological units. There may also be pertinent distribution of contrastive syllables into grammatical units (K. Pike, 1967:384-85).
 Merrifield (1963:2) notes that syllables with contrastive tone do not occur poststress in Palantla Chinantec, although syllables which occur prestress do have contrastive tone.
 In Halang of Viet Nam (Cooper, 1966:93), there are restrictions as to the type of syllables which may occur in the first-syllable slot of a word. For example, a syllable in that position has only one initial consonant, although the syllable in the second-syllable slot of the word may have one, two, or three presyllabic consonants.

In Marinahua of Peru (E.V. Pike and Scott, 1962:2) the contrastive syllable type CCV never occurs in the initial slot of a phonological word.

In Itonama of Bolivia (Liccardi and Grimes, 1968:39) a syllable with a final consonant never occurs in the final slot of a word.

According to Siertsema (1959:385-87), no verb in Yoruba begins with a vowel, whereas all nouns of native origin begin with a vowel. That is, the distribution of the syllable type V versus CV into grammatical units is pertinent.

3. PHONOLOGICAL WORD LEVEL

The phonological word is distributed into the next higher level. The phonological word is sometimes called "stress group" and sometimes called "foot".

In this paper I will discuss the phonological word level and phonological phrase level separately. K. Pike includes them both under "stress group" (1967:392-402) perhaps because numerous languages do not have both levels. In his *Intonation of American English*, however, K. Pike was writing both "normal" and "partially suppressed" stress (1945:vii, 87-96). Presumably he was reacting to the hierarchy of rhythm waves, although at the time (1945) the phonological hierarchy had not yet been described. From my point of view, his normal stress is simultaneously the nucleus of the phonological phrase and the nucleus of the phonological word. His "partially suppressed stress" (he also calls it "partially reduced stress" 1945:vii) is the nucleus of a phonological word when it occurs in the phonological phrase margin.

3.1. *The phonological word nucleus*

The nucleus of the word is more commonly called the stressed syllable, but the contrastive features with which the stressed syllable is marked vary from language to language. Whenever there is a phonetic feature which occurs once in every word, but not twice, that feature is probably marking the word nucleus.

In some languages the predominant feature marking the word nucleus may be:

(a) High pitch. For example, Ganja of Papua New Guinea (E.V. Pike, 1964:121).

(b) Length of vowel. For example, English (Denes and Pinson, 1963:136), Polish (Lehiste, 1970:133), French (Delattre, 1964:44), Chontal of

Mexico (Turner, 1967:30).

(c) Length of consonant. For example, Eastern Popoloca (Kalstrom and E.V. Pike, 1968:16,17).

(d) Articulatory energy. Delattre says (1964:44) that the stressed syllable of English and German "owes its prominence to a larger expanse of articulatory energy... Not only do vowel intensity, vowel duration, and vowel pitch (fundamental frequency) play a part but also consonant intensity and consonant closure duration..."

(e) A bundle of features including some of the above with, perhaps, the addition of vigorous articulation, loudness, preaspirated stops, etc. Malécot (1963:92) says that pitch, duration, and loudness mark word stress in Luiseño.

3.2. *Contrastive words (the feature mode)*

There are various features with which phonological words may be contrasted. For example, stress, tone, length, nasalization, breathiness, laryngealization. The emic phonological word may be taken as a whole, in which case stress, nasalization, etc., are contrastive features of the word. Or, the predominant feature which contrasts one phonological word with another may be considered to be an eme (K. Pike 1967:407-08), in which case stress, tone, length, nasalization, etc., are considered to be suprasegmental phonemes.

1) One word type may contrast with another by the placement of the nucleus, that is, by the placement of the stressed syllable for example, as in English, and in Spanish. Also in Batad Ifugao of the Philippines (Newell, 1970:112), and Tarahumara of Mexico (Burgess, 1970:52).

2) Tone may be a contrastive feature which distinguishes one word type from another. When tone is a contrastive feature of the word, the contrast occurs on one specific part of the word, usually on the stressed syllable. The pitch of the other syllable is predictable, varies freely, or is conditioned by intonation.

(a) Pame of Mexico (Gibson, 1956:258), Fasu of Papua New Guinea (May and Loeweke 1965:94, 95), Gurung of Nepal (K. Pike, 1970) all have tone contrasting on the stressed syllable.

(b) Yotsukura (1967) describes Japanese as a system with word tone. Some words have no high syllable and other words have one syllable (only one) which is innately high. The syllable following an innate high must be low, so when listening for an emic high tone, a person may find it easiest to listen for the fall. (But if the innately high syllable is the last syllable for the word, there is no fall.) There is a complex system of intonation which raises some innately low tones.

(c) In Terena of Brazil the word types are distinguished by a syllable with high tone which, in some environments, is immediately followed by a long consonant versus a syllable with low tone which occurs with a long vowel. Bendor-Samuel calls them Type A stress versus Type B stress (1963:107-08).

3) Length.

Eastern Popoloca of Mexico. Either CV· or C·V occurs in each stressed syllable, and only in the stressed syllable (Kalstrom and E.V. Pike, 1968: 17,18).

4) Nasalization.

When nasalization is a contrastive feature of the word, the contrast usually occurs on one part of the word only. For example on the stressed syllable, on the first syllable, or on the last syllable. The nasalization of the other syllables is predictable, or varies freely. The emically nasalized syllable may condition any contiguous or noncontiguous syllable whose intervening consonants are /ʔ/, /h/, or resonants. But emically nasalized syllables usually do not condition noncontiguous vowels which have an intervening stop or fricative (but the intervening stop itself may become prenasalized).

Examples of languages with nasalization as a contrastive feature on the word level:

(a) Coatzospan Mixtec of Mexico. The contrast occurs on the last syllable of the word. That word always has the second person familiar as one of its components of meaning (E.V. Pike and Small, 1973:124).

(b) Ostuacan Zoque of Mexico. The contrast occurs on the first syllable of the word. That word always has the second person as one of its components of meaning (Engel and Longacre, 1963:334, footnote 6).

(c) Terena of Brazil. The contrast occurs on the first syllable, and the word involved always has the first person as one of its components of meaning (Bendor-Samuel, 1960:350). Bendor-Samuel treats nasalization as a prosody.

(d) In Warao of Venezuela a nasalized vowel or consonant conditions vowels to the right. The conditioning passes through /w, y, h/ but is stopped by other consonants (Osborn, 1966:111-12).

(e) Kaiwa of Brazil. The contrast occurs on the stressed syllable with nasalization conditioned or fluctuating on the nonstressed syllables (Bridgeman, 1961:332). (For a description of a slightly different system of word-level nasalization, perhaps a different dialect of Kaiwa, see Harrison and Taylor, 1971).

(f) In Shiriana of Brazil and Venezuela all the vowels of a nasal word are nasal, even when the intervening consonant is a stop or fricative (Migliazza and Grimes, 1961:35).

5) Ballistic articulation versus controlled articulation.

One word type may contrast with another word type by the ballistic versus controlled articulation of the stressed syllable. A ballistic syllable is characterized by a forceful beginning followed by rapid decrescendo. The syllable may end in voicelessness. When the ballistic syllable is checked, the final stop may be heavily aspirated. In a controlled syllable, there is less decrescendo, less voicelessness, less aspiration. If the syllables also have contrastive tone, the allotones of ballistic syllables are different from those in controlled syllables. Also, a controlled syllable may be longer than a ballastic one.

In some of the Chinantec languages of Mexico, each stressed syllable has either ballistic or controlled articulation. Because the contrast occurs only on stressed syllables, I prefer to handle it as a contrast of word-types rather than of syllables. See Merrifield's description of Palantla Chinantec (1963:3) and Foris' description of Sochiapan Chinantec (1973:235).

6) Breathiness versus nonbreathiness.

One word type may be contrasted with another by a breathy versus a nonbreathy vowel whose occurrence is restricted to one slot in the word.

Breathy vowels may have audible breathiness, or the contrast between breathiness and nonbreathiness may be "some type of clear versus hollow quality caused by a smaller or larger throat cavity made by a visible raising or lowering of the larynx. The 'breathy' vowel in some of the languages lowers the pitch, leading to conditioned allotones" (K. Pike, 1970:153).

Gurung of Nepal has contrast between breathiness versus nonbreathiness. The contrast is restricted to the first syllable of the word (K. Pike, 1970:155). See also (Glover, 1969:51).

7) Laryngealization versus nonlaryngealization.

In Sedang of Viet Nam there is contrast between laryngealized versus nonlaryngealized words. Smith (1968:56-58) has described it in relation to the vowel, but the contrast occurs only on a stressed syllable, therefore I prefer to handle it as a contrastive feature of the word.

8) Ideophonic versus nonideophonic words.

Migliazza and Grimes (1961:35) describe ideophonic words in Shiriana of Brazil and Venezuela as "usually laryngealized or breathy in relation to overall voice quality... highly conventionalized and specialized in meaning."

58

9) Simple nuclei versus complex nuclei.

Phonological words may contrast by simple nuclei versus complex nuclei.
A word with a simple nucleus is one whose nucleus consists of one syllable. A
word with a complex nucleus is one whose nucleus consists of two or more
syllables.

(a) A complex nucleus may be marked with double stress.
     In some dialects of English there are words with complex nuclei. For
     example: ´new ´born versus ´newness, or ´newsman; ´hand ´made versus
     ´handmaid; ´bob ´white versus ´bobsled. Notice that ´bob ´white is not a
     sequence of two words since it contrasts with ´Bob White

(b) A complex nucleus may be marked by consonant allophones. For
     example, in Ayutla Mixtec of Mexico, a stop which occurs nucleus-
     medially is preceded by [h] ; a continuant which occurs nucleus-medially
     is lengthened (Pankratz and E.V. Pike, 1967:288).

(c) A complex nucleus may have either contiguous or noncontiguous
     stressed syllables.
     Words contrast with one another in accordance with the different stress
     patterns. (In some languages they also contrast with words which have no
     stressed syllables.) When there is a high percentage of words with
     complex nuclei, contrasting by the stress pattern, these languages are
     sometimes called "multiple stress" languages. When the percentage is
     lower, the term "multiple stress" is less apt to be applied.
     For examples of languages with contrastive stress patterns within the
     word see: Campa (K. Pike and Kindberg, 1956), Arabela (Rich, 1963),
     Chuave (Swick, 1966), Waffa (Stringer and Hotz, 1971:46), Barua
     (Lloyd and Healey, 1970:38).

(d) Alternation between words with a simple nucleus versus words with a
     complex nucleus.
     For example, in English ´intonation; alternates with inton´ation; ´sar´dine
     alternates with sar´dine. In words which optionally have a complex
     nucleus, it is the second stressed syllable which becomes the nucleus of a
     phonological phrase (K. Pike, 1945:77).

3.3. *Variants of words (the manifestation mode).*

An emic word has variants according to the syllable types which are
distributed in it. For example, the word type with stress on the last syllable
includes the English words: *routine, indeed, canoe, confess.* The emic word
type is the same in all, but the words have variants differing by the syllable
types. They are: [CV'CVC], [VC'CVC], [CV'CV], [CVC'CVC].

The emic words may also have variants differing by pitch in accordance with their distribution in a specific emic phrase. For example, when *canoe* is distributed in the /° 3-2/ phrase, the pitch is [$-\smile$]. When *canoe* is distributed in a /° 2-4/ phrase, the pitch is [$-\frown$].

Emic words also have variants differing by full stress versus reduced or partially suppressed stress in accordance with their distribution in the nucleus of an emic phrase versus their distribution in the margin of an emic phrase. For example *canoe* has reduced stress in *The canoe is ° big.* But *canoe* has full stress in *I saw a ca °noe.* (K. Pike, 1945:vi,vii, 27-28).

When trying to hear the contrastive features which identify word stress, it is often necessary to put the word in the margin of an emic phrase, since, if the word is in the nucleus of an emic phrase, the contrastive feature of phrase stress may be superimposed on that of word stress.

For example, when heard in isolation *'permit verus per 'mit* seem to have word stress indicated by high tone. When, however, they are said in the following sentences (in which there is emphatic stress on *say*, and *'permit* and *per 'mit* are in the margin of the phrase), length is the predominant feature identifying the word stress:

I didn't 'Say 'permit.
I didn't 'Say per 'mit.

3.4. *Distribution of words*

In some languages there is a restriction in the distribution of emic word types. For example, in some languages only words with a final stress may occur in certain emic phrases. In Spanish the sales boys hawking their wares on the street call, *chic 'le* 'chewing gum' with an upglide and stress on the second syllable, instead of *'chicle* with the normal stress on the first syllable. They say *dul 'ce* 'candy' with an upglide, instead of *'dulce*. Also, when calling to someone at a distance, the Spanish name *Cata 'rina* is pronounced with stress on the last syllable, *Catari 'na*.

3.5. *Sequences of phonological words*

A phonological word is a rhythm wave made up of syllables which in turn are rhythm waves made up of phonemes. A phonological word may be one of a sequence of words, making up a phonological phrase, or a pause group. In some languages the phonological word is a unit of time. That is, there is a tendency for words with only two syllables to take as much time as words with more syllables. For example, Molinos Mixtec (Hunter and E.V. Pike,

1969:24), and numerous languages of Papua New Guinea (E.V. Pike, 1964:124).

Since the phonological word is a unit, it should be possible to determine how many phonological words occur in a specific phonological phrase or pause group.

In a language which has only words with simple nuclei, the number of words in a stream of speech can usually be determined by counting the nuclei. In a language with complex nuclei, however, there may not be one syllable of the word which is more prominent than the others. In such a language (probably one with both contiguous and noncontiguous stressed syllables), it may be possible to determine the number of words in a stream of speech by counting the borders between words (K. Pike, 1967:420). That is, in such a language the borders between words are usually more easily identified than are the borders in a language with simple nuclei.

The nucleus of the normal rhythm wave (K. Pike, 1962) which is a phonological word is apt to be long, loud, and perhaps has high pitch. In the prenucleus of the word, the syllables may be faster than those in the post nucleus. Between the beginning of the word and the nucleus there is usually crescendo. From the nucleus to the end of the word, there is usually decrescendo. Therefore the border between the rhythm waves may be marked by a speed change from slow to faster, a pitch change from lower to higher, a change from lenisness to fortisness.

In some languages the border between phonological words may also be determined:

(a) By the allophones of phonemes.
   In Hihgland Chontal of Mexico (Turner, 1967:30) the phoneme /k/ has an allophone /kʰ/ which occurs only in word-final position.
   In Rawang on the Burma-Tibetan border, resonants are lengthened and stops are unreleased when in word-final position (Morse, 1963:29).

(b) By the distribution of phonemes.
   In Bhojpuri of India (Trammell, 1971:135,137) any vowel may occur in syllable-final position, but four of the vowels do not occur in word-final position. Also, any consonant may occur in syllable-initial position, but there are three consonants that do not occur in word-initial position.

(c) By the distribution of consonant clusters.
   In Itonama of Bolivia (Liccardi and Grimes, 1968:39), a word always precedes a consonant cluster beginning with /s/.

(d) By the insertion of a lenis glottal stop.
   In Shiriana (Migliazza and Grimes, 1961:35-36), and in Rawang (Morse, 1963:29).

(e) By a slight up-step in pitch.

In Waffa (Stringer and Hotz, 1971:46).
(f)   By the distribution of the nuclei.
      In a language with simple nuclei only, a border must occur between two
      nuclei.

When a language has words with simple nuclei, and there are no phonetic
criteria for determining the border (especially in fast speech), K. Pike
(1967:385) speaks of a syllable in double function. That is, a single syllable
both closes the first phonological word and starts the second.

When a border cannot be determined by phonetic criteria, it is helpful to
note the potential pause points, or to notice the distribution of the
morphemes, or group of morphemes involved. If a specific sequence can
occur at the beginning, at the end, and in the middle of an utterance, it
probably begins and ends with a word border. But a border should not be
placed in such a way that a contiguous morpheme is surrounded by borders
when it has no stress and never occurs in isolation. For a good discussion of
border phenomena, see K. Pike (1947:159-68).

The phonetic phenomena which identify the borders between words may
be considered to be contrastive features of the word. For example, the
allophones of phonemes which are conditioned by their place in the word are
contrastive features of the word (K. Pike, 1967:407-09).

Or, the phonetic phenomena which identify borders between words may
be considered to be emes. If so, as a bundle they are often called plus
juncture, or sometimes they are called internal open juncture. Lehiste has
made an acoustic study of plus juncture (1960). See also, Hoard (1966).

4. OTHER LEVELS BELOW THE PAUSE-GROUP LEVEL

All languages have a phoneme level, most have a syllable level, a pause-group
level, and a level between the syllable and pause-group.

In the literature it is not always easy to equate a level of one language with
that of another since the labels vary from one description to another. Word
level has also been called "foot", "rhythm group", and sometimes "stress
group". Phrase level may be called "stress group", and also "contour". Phrase
level is also the name under which the pause group is sometimes described.

4.1. *Non-English phrase-level examples*

Some languages have two levels, both a word and a phrase level, between the syllable and pause-group levels. For example, Sherpa (Gordon, 1970:205), Shiriana (Migliazza and Grimes, 1961:36).

The phonological phrase of Tamang contrast by various juncture features (Hari, Taylor, and K. Pike, 1970:92, 111).

In Shiriana (Migliazza and Grimes, 1961:36) the phonological phrases (called by them "contour") in a sequence of phonological phrases, all receive approximately the same amount of time. Therefore when a phonological phrase contains several phonological words, those words are pronounced rapidly. When a phonological phrase contains only a word or two, those words are pronounced slowly. The phrase stress is louder than word stress; it occurs on the same syllable as the word stress of the last phonological word of the phrase.

In Comanche units are contrasted by rhythm (Smalley, 1953:298-99). The level involved is not clearly identified. I am assuming it to be the phrase level.

Some languages have only one level between the syllable and the pause-group level. For example, Coatzospan Mixtec has a word-phrase level. This level has glottalized versus nonglottalized word-phrase units as well as nasal versus oral word-phrase units (E.V. Pike and Small, 1973:122-26).

Arabella of Peru has a level between syllable and word (Rich, 1963:201-02). Each unit begins with a stressed syllable and contains from one to five syllables.

4.2. *The phonological phrase of English*

K. Pike's *The intonation of American English* (1945) was written prior to the development of tagmemic phonology. His goal was "the isolation and listing of as many of these contrastive characteristics of intonation as possible" (1945:1), and "the postulation of such an intonation theory, with its relationship to pause, rhythm, and voice quality" (1945:19).

In this section I have, for the most part, taken his data and have restated it according to my understanding of the emic phonological phrase of American English. Some of the data I have included under phonological word (the introduction of Section 3, and 3.2, subdivision 9). Some of the data I include under contrastive pause groups (Section 5.1).

Normally in American English the phrase nucleus (the stressed syllable) is relatively long. Syllables preceding the nucleus are pronounced relatively rapidly. Therefore in a sequence of phonological phrases within an emic pause group, the border between phonological phrases is indicated by the change of speed from slow (the end of one phonological phrase) to fast (the beginning of the second). This border between phonological phrases has been called by

K. Pike, the "intonation break" (1945:187, footnote 108).

In the following example the phrase border comes between the words *first* and *then*.

The ˈsoldier ˈcame ˈfirst ˈthen the po ˈliceman
3 °2 4-3: 3 °2 4//

(1 is high intoneme; 4 is low intoneme; ° indicates phrase stress; a hyphen indicates length with decrescendo or a glide from one pitch to another; a colon indicates the phrase border; an apostrophe indicates word stress; / indicates tentative pause; // indicates final pause.)

When the phrase stress occurs on the last syllable of the phrase, the border may be signalled by decrescendo, as in

ˈyes ˈI'll ˈgo
°4-3; °2 4-3//

The preceding example was a sequence of two phrases within one emic pause group. It would become a sequence of two pause groups merely by inserting a medial pause, as in

ˈyes ˈI'll ˈgo
°4-3/ °2 4-3//

A phonological phrase which contains several phonological words may easily become (when spoken more slowly) a sequence of phonological phrases. The following with several phonological words is only one phonological phrase:

The ˈolder ˈsister was ˈquarrelsome.
3 °2 4//

As a sequence of three phrases:

The ˈolder ˈsister was ˈquarrelsome.
3 °2 3: °2 3: 3 °2 4//

As a sequence of two pause groups:

The ˈolder ˈsister was ˈquarrelsome.
3 °2 3: °2 3/ 3 °2 4//

The border between two phrases may be indefinite. A syllable may serve both as the end point of one phrase, and as the beginning of the second. Such a syllable is short and without decrescendo.

A phonological phrase may at the same time be an emic pause group, as in

The   ˇcaptain   ˙went   home
3   ° 2-4//

When an emic pause group consists of only one phonological phrase, K. Pike has called it a "simple rhythm unit" (1945:vii, 34). When a sequence of phonological phrases occurs within an emic pause group, K. Pike has called it a "complex rhythm unit" (1945:vii, 37).

The contrastive features which mark the nucleus of a phonological phrase are usually more intensified than those which mark the nucleus of the phonological word. The phrase nucleus is sometimes called "sentence stress." It is usually longer than other syllables, but in English it may be short when extreme loudness is added in certain contrastive phrases. For example

´What   ˇis   it? (K. Pike, 1945:86).
3   ° 2   4//

The syllable with phrase stress usually starts with the highest pitch of the phrase, but in certain emic phrases the following pitches may be higher.

Will   you   have   ˙tea?
3   ° 2-1

In certain emic phrases the stressed syllable may start with the lowest pitch.

Is   he   ˇgoing   to   ˙Boston?
3   ° 4   1/

That is, the phrase nucleus is signalled by a combination of length, loudness, and high pitch. In some emic phrases, one feature is predominant, in other phrases a different feature is predominant.

The phrase nucleus usually occurs on the syllable where word stress also occurs, but when a syllable is to receive special attention, the phrase stress may be placed on that syllable even though it does not have innate word stress (K. Pike, 1945:84).

It's in   the 'book.
3   °2-4   4//

A phonological phrase has a complex nucleus if it has two or more phrase stresses within the one phonological phrase (K. Pike, 1945:39, 61).

Following is a pair of examples. The word *big* in example (a) has phrase stress but it has no decrescendo signalling phrase juncture, neither is it as long as *big* in example (b). Example (a), then, is one phrase with the complex nucleus *big man*. Example (b) is a sequence of two phrases; *big* is the nucleus of the first phrase, and *man* is the nucleus of the second.

(a) *'He's a   big 'man.*
     3   °2   °2-4//
(b) *'He's a   big 'man.*
     3   °2-2:°2-4//

A phonological phrase may also have a complex margin. (This is analogous to a consonant cluster which is a complex margin of a syllable.) An example of a phonological phrase with a complex margin is,

'This one, he 'said.
°2   4:   4   4//

In the previous example *he said* is a complex margin and not a phonological phrase since it has no phrase stress. It is not postnuclear in a simple phonological phrase, since it is separated from the phrase stress by a phrase juncture. K. Pike calls it a "weak rhythm unit" (1945:39).

A complex margin may both precede and follow the phrase stress (K. Pike, 1945:40) as in,

I said--I will 'not 'go.
2   : 3   °2-4: 4//

Contrastive phrases in English are for the most part made up of combinations of four intonemes, 1 (high), 2, 3, 4 (low). Between the nucleus of the contour and the end of the phrase, there may be any of at least twenty-two contrastive contours (K. Pike, 1945:44-65). Those with falling glides have the general meaning of 'selective attention': those with rising glides have the general meaning of 'incompleteness' or 'needing supplementation'. The attitude of the speaker is shown more specifically by means of the starting and ending points of the contour. These meanings may be further modified by combinations of the falling and rising glides.

A few examples follow:

´Miss ·´Hill (incompleteness)
3   °3-2
´Miss ´Hill (surprise or unbelief added to incompleteness)
3   °3-1/
´Miss ´Hill (sternness added to incompleteness)
3   °3-3/
´Miss ´Hill (formality added to selective attention)
3   °3-4/
´Will you ´have ´tea? (politeness added to incompleteness)
3   °2-1/
´I'll ´try. (deliberation added to selective attention)
3   °2-4-3/

There are also level contours which have a meaning of 'nonfinality' and 'unification' (K. Pike, 1945:62-65).

Contrast may also occur between the beginning of the phonological phrase and the stressed syllable. The pitch may be relatively level at one of four heights, it may start low and rise steadily, or start high and drop steadily (K. Pike, 1945:66-68).

Phonological phrases may also contrast by vowel length as *long* in,

The ˈlittle ˈboy ˈwent a ˈlo·ng ˈway.
3   °2-3: 3   °2   4//

Phonological phrases may contrast by length of consonant, as in,

´Don't ´d-o ´that!
°2-2: °2   4//

For a discussion of further contrasts, see K. Pike (1945:97-105).

4.3. *Variants of phonological phrases (the manifestation mode)*

(1) A phonological phrase has variants dependent on the number of words which occur in it. For example, in English,

'John.   versus 'John   'went 'home.
°2-4//   °2-4   4//

(2) The shape of the contour varies in accordance with the placement of word stress. That is, in accordance with the phonological word type which occurs in it. For example, both of the following words are said with the same emic phrase, °2-4, but the shape of the contours differ.

'always   versus   ab 'surd
°2-4   3 °2-4

(3) The emic phrases have variants in accordance with the placement of the phrase stress.

I 'have a 'red 'dress.
°2   4//
or: 3   °2   4//
or: 3   °2-4//

These are not different contrastive phrases since the meaning of °2-4 remains the same, namely, 'put your attention on this word'.

(4) Phonological phrases have variants in accordance with their distribution in the type of pause group. For example, in English a phrase with falling tones will glide lower if it occurs at the end of a final pause than it will if occurring at the end of a tentative pause (K. Pike, 1945:104-05).

4.4. Distribution of phrases

There may be limited distribution of phonological phrases. For example, in English the rising contours and contours falling to tone 3 do not occur at the end of a final pause group. Also, level contours rarely occur at the end of a final pause group (K. Pike, 1945:152-55).

5. THE PAUSE-GROUP LEVEL

The chief characteristic of the pause-group level is that it is a rhythm wave (composed of lesser rhythm waves) which occurs between pauses. For a description of normal rhythm waves in general, see K. Pike (1962), and see

68

his "Abdominal pulse types in some Peruvian languages" (1957) in which he describes the sharp difference between the rhythm waves of four different languages of Peru.

5.1. *Contrastive pause groups (the feature mode)*

The most common contrastive units of an emic pause group are final versus nonfinal pause. The final pause group usually has a relaxation of the muscular movements with which the pause group ends, and is often accompanied by downdrift of pitch. The nonfinal pause group is usually accompanied by tenseness, a lack of relaxation in the muscular movements with which the pause group ends, and a lack of downdrift of pitch. The rhythm wave as a whole, however, varies from language to language. For example, in Rocoroibo Tarahumara the vowel of the first nonstressed syllable in a pause group is lengthened (Burgess, 1970:59).

The following languages have been described as having nonfinal versus final pause groups, but the actual phonetic manifestation varies from language to language. English (but not described in terms of the phonological hierarchy, K. Pike, 1945:31), Kunjen (Sommer, 1969:16-20), Golin (Bunn, 1970:5-6), Rocoroibo Tarahumara (Burgess, 1970:61), Selepet (McElhanon, 1970:6-8), Manambu (Allen and Hurd, 1972:42). In the above articles the pause-group level has sometimes been called "phonological phrase", but the unit occurs between pauses in all of them.

Borman chose to describe the terminals of Cofan as emes rather than the pause-group unit as a whole. He has phrase-final juncture versus nonfinal juncture (1962:59). Also, Grimes describes Huichol (1959:226, 230) and Orr describes Quichua (1962:63-64) as having three contrastive terminal junctures.

In a number of languages, contrastive pause groups are the means for signalling the attitude of the speaker. That is, for indicating intonation-like meanings.

For example, in Arabela a rising intonation over the whole phrase is used in narration; strong decrescendo, usually to voicelessness, shows hesitation; the whole pause group in high falsetto shows surprise (Rich, 1963: 203-04).

In Eastern Popoloca in the anger-pause group, the last syllable is long and ends in a lenis (instead of a fortis) glottal stop. Optionally, the anger-pause group begins with an alveolar click (Kalstrom and E.V. Pike, 1968:29).

For a description of other emic pause groups also used for indicating the attitude of the speaker see: Fasu (May and Loeweke, 1965:95, 96), Kunjen (Sommer, 1969:16-27), Batad Ifugao (Newell, 1970:113-16), Golin (Bunn,

1970:5-6), Rocoroibo Tarahumara (Burgess, 1970:59-62), Selepet
(McElhanon, 1970:6-12).

In the following three languages, the intonation is described in terms of
the contrastive features of pitch, intonemes, rather than by the contrastive
pause group as a whole: Huastec (Larsen and E.V. Pike, 1949:269-73),
Mazahua (E.V. Pike, 1951:37-39), Huichol (Grimes, 1959:227-30),
Totontepec Mixe (Crawford, 1963:144-48), Kunimaipa (Pence, 1964).

5.2. *Variants of pause groups (the manifestation mode)*

An emic pause group has variants (K. Pike, 1967:403) dependent upon the
number and kind of lower level units which occur in it. It also has variants in
accordance with the speech style with which it occurs.

A pause group has variants in accordance with its distribution into the
higher levels of the phonological hierarchy, into the phonological paragraph,
for example. That is, decrescendo starts further back in the pause group when
it occurs near the end of a long paragraph than it does when occurring near
the beginning of a paragraph, or when it occurs in a short paragraph.

6. LEVELS ABOVE THE PAUSE GROUP

There are other emic units which are parts of levels higher than the pause
group (K. Pike, 1967:403-05), but not many have been described for specific
languages.

The breath group is described for Batad Ifugao by Newell (1970:115), and
for Selepet by McElhanon (1970:5).

A phonological sentence is described for Mazatec by E. Pike
(1967:314-15), and Sherpa by Gordon (1970:206).

McMahon describes seven phonological levels for Cora (1967), Powlison
describes eight for Yagua (1971). Turner describes eight for Highland Chontal
(1967).

7. THE PHONEME

The phoneme, the unit on the lowest level of the phonological hierarchy, is
described in relation to the other phonological levels and to the other
hierarchies by K. Pike in *Language* (1967:294-344).

It is K. Pike's book *Phonemics* (1947), however, which gives the

70

techniques for analyzing a language in relation to its phonemes. The following lists some of the points covered. (a) The need for contrast and how to recognize it (73-77, 80-81). (b) Allophones (called "submembers"), and how to be alert for and recognize them (84-96, 116-19). (c) The basis for decision (called "interpretation procedures") in the problem area of sounds which in some environments are vowels and in other environments are consonants; and the basis for decisions concerning sequences of sounds which in some languages may be a sequence of phonemes, and in other languages may make up one phoneme, etc. (128-49). (d) Suggestions for recognizing juncture (called "border phenomena") (159-68). (e) The analysis of fluctuating pronunciation (122-25). (f) The analysis of tone (105-111).

For more than twenty-five years a succession of students have been studying from K. Pike's *Phonemics*. Their subsequent work on the field shows that the areas in which they most frequently have trouble are (a) portmanteau phones, and bidirectional fusion, (b) partial overlap, (c) displaced contrast, (d) archiphoneme.

The desired end-product of an analysis is well-defined units — particles. It is the wave characteristic of language, the rhythmic movement of the vocal apparatus, that causes units to be modified by their environments, and, at times, causes a sequence of two or more units to be fused into one phone. (See K. Pike's "Language as particle, wave, and field" (1959), and also 1967:308-09, 545-50.)

By looking at language from a field point of view, the fact that there are sequences which have been fused may be recognized and the fused units identified. Looking from a field point of view, we note the symmetry of consonant clusters and of vowel clusters (becoming aware of the clusters which are lacking also). We note the distribution of phonemes into the various slots in the word. We note the phoneme classes which occur and those which do not occur in those slots. We note the lack of this or that phoneme which would be in some specific environment if the class which occurred in that environment were complete. We note the distribution of consonants in relation to vowels. We note the classes which occur, and the absence of an expected phoneme. We note the unique occurrence of a phone. We note the unexpected phone — if all were symmetrical it would not be in that environment.

1) A portmanteau phone (caused by the wave characteristic of language) is one etic sound which is emically two phonemes. A unique phone, the one not a part of a symmetrical pattern may turn out to be a portmanteau phone. When the units which make up the portmanteau phone are recognized, their occurrence should help to make symmetrical one of the nonsymmetrical patterns. K. Pike (1947:138-40) discusses "interpreting single segments as

sequences of phonemes..." and he lists some of the phones which at times prove to be portmanteau phones: nasalized vowels, retroflexed vocoids, laryngealized vocoids, syllabic resonants, etc. See K. Pike (1967:317-18) for discussion of a portmanteau phone.

Following are some examples of portmanteau phones.

Harris (1951:92) describes a flapped nasal which occurs in some environments in some dialects of American English (as in, for example, *painting*) as actualizing the sequence /nt/.

In Quiotepec Chinantec the sequence /mï/ is actualized as a syllabic bilabial nasal (Robbins, 1961:245).

In Ayutla Mixtec the sequence /ae/ is actualized as [ae] when following an alveopalatal consonant (Pankratz and E.V. Pike, 1967:289).

In Walmatjari of Australia the sequence /lu/ and the sequence /ŋu/ are optionally actualized as a rounded lateral and a rounded velar nasal respectively when occurring nonstressed in word-final position (Hudson and Richards, 1969:179).

In Barua of Papua New Guinea the sequence /ty/ is actualized as /ž/ when following a vowel (Lloyd and Healy, 1970: 35).

2) Bidirectional partial fusion (also called "reciprocal conditioning") is also the result of the wave movement of speech. There is anticipation of the articulation of the second segment of the sequence with a delayed decay of the first. This is similar to a portmanteau, but the fusion of the two segments is complete in a portmanteau phone, and it is not complete in bidirectional partial fusion (K. Pike, 1967:317, 548-49).

In Kiowa (my analysis) [æ] fluctuating with [ɛ] occurs only following a palatalized velar. A palatalized velar occurs only when preceding [æ] or [ɛ] There has been reciprocal conditioning of the phonemes in the sequence /ka/.

3) Partial overlap. A phoneme is not a physically unchanging absolute. The allophones with which a phoneme is manifested may have considerable variation from one environment to another. In fact, as long as the contrast in each environment is preserved, a phoneme may have an allophone in one environment which is homophonous with the allophone of another phoneme occurring in a different environment. Under those circumstances, the environment becomes part of the contrastive features with which the phonemes are distinguished.

When a phoneme is manifested by an allophone in one environment, which is homophonous with an allophone of a different phoneme occurring in a different environment, the two phonemes are said to be in "partial overlap".

For a discussion of this phenomenon, see Bloch (1941), Harris (1951:65), and K. Pike (1967:299-300).

Following are examples of languages in which partial overlap occurs.

In Sierra Popoluca a voiceless alveolar nasal is allophone of /h/ when following /n/, but it is allophone of /t/ when preceding /n/. For a discussion, showing examples and contrast with other phonemes, see Elson (1947:15).

In Amuzgo a voiceless lateral is allophone of /h/ when preceding /l/; a similar voiceless lateral is allophone of /l/ when preceding /k/ (Bauernschmidt, 1965:477).

In Barua, a voiceless bilabial stop is allophone of / ʔ /when preceding /p/ or /m/; but it is allophone of /p/ in other environments (Lloyd and Healey, 1970:34).

4) Displaced contrast. When one phoneme is in contrast with another, various features may be part of that contrast. Usually we think of one of the features as the predominant feature, and the others as redundant. The predominant feature usually occurs as part of the phoneme itself. The redundant features may be part of the environment. Sometimes, however, the predominant feature is lost and the redundant features take over. When that occurs, I have called it "displaced contrast".

One of the best known examples of displaced contrast occurs in the dialects of English which have voicing versus voicelessness as the predominant feature contrasting / b, d, g/ versus /p, t, k/. When prepause (in those dialects) /b, d, g/ become voiceless and the contrast between the two series of stops is carried by the environment. That is, the contrast is maintained by the lengthened vocoid preceding the voiced phonemes versus the short vocoid preceding the voiceless phonemes. Similarly, the /d/ and /t/ in *rider* versus *writer* are distinguished by the allophonic length of the syllable nucleus which they follow. (see also Harris, 1951:70, 71).

In Quecha of Bolivia, there is a contrast between a velar stop and a back-velar stop. The vowel /i/ becomes [e] when contiguous to /ḳ/. When in syllable-final position, both /k/ and /ḳ/ become a voiceless velar fricative. In that environment the two phonemes /k/ and /ḳ/ are distinguished by the allophones of /i/. That is, the sequence /ik/ is actualized as [ix] ; the sequence /iḳ/ is actualized as [ex] (Peter Landerman, private communication).

In Yatzachi Zapotec there are three contrasting syllables with the tones: high, mid, and low. Pitch is the predominant contrastive feature, but there is a redundant feature in that a syllable with high tone is shorter than a syllable with mid or low tone. When a monosyllabic word with mid or high tone occurs in phrase-final position, the pitch of the two syllables may be the same (especially when following a syllable with low tone). That is, although the syllables have a mid-pitched short vocoid and a mid-pitched long vocoid, the emic distinction between the syllables is high tone versus a mid tone (E.V. Pike, 1948:167).

5) Archiphoneme. Two phonemes which contrast in most environments may loose that contrast in some specific environment. A phone which occurs in that environment and is phonetically similar to both phonemes, and is in complementary distribution with both, is called an archiphoneme. An archiphoneme is not more similar to one of the pair of phonemes than it is to the other.

For further discussion of an archiphoneme, see K. Pike, (1947:141 called "under-differentiated phonemes"), and (1967:300-01, 359-60). See Hockett (1955:164-66) for his summary of the use of an archiphoneme by the Prague school.

In some dialects of English there are less syllable nuclei which contrast when preceding /r/, than there are when preceding other consonants. For example, the vowels which are in contrast in the words *beat* versus *bit, boat* versus *bought*, etc., do not contrast when preceding /r/. That is, the vowels in the syllable nuclei of *beer* and *bore* are archiphonemes. See Lehiste (1964:78-114) for a discussion of the allophones of English vowels when preceding /r/.

In Mantjiltjara of Australia the contrast between /t, n, l/ and /t, n, l/ is neutralized when in utterance-initial position. An archiphoneme, which has the tongue in a semi-retroflexed position, is used in that environment (Marsh, 1969:135).

In Cham of Viet Nam the contrast between /s/ and /h/ is neutralized when occurring in a word-final position following /i/. The archiphoneme which occurs in that environment is a voiceless velar fricative (Blood, 1967:19).

8. BOOKS ON THE THEORY OF TAGMEMIC PHONOLOGY

8.1. *K. Pike's* Language

Tagmemic theory was first set forth in 1954 (K. Pike, 1967 [first edition, Part I, 1954]). This Part I dealt with language as behavior, nonverbal behavior, emic units of behavior, the morpheme, and the tagmeme itself. Phonology as related to tagmemic theory was not in print until 1955 when Part II was published (K. Pike, 1967 [first edition, Part II, 1955]). Many of the insights for tagmemic phonology started before that, however. In fact, many of the insights for tagmemic theory itself started with phonology. (It was the awareness that a phoneme was a definite unit that caused K. Pike to look for a similar unit of grammar — eventually he posited the tagmeme.) That is, seeds of tagmemic theory can be seen in works published earlier than 1955. For this reason, some of these early works are referred to in this chapter. Some articles referred to, even though not following the tagmemic model, provide good examples of contrastive units above the phoneme, of fusion, etc.

The basic theory of tagmemic phonology is given in chapters 8 and 9 of *Language* (K. Pike, 1967, 290-423; esp. 294-344, 364-409). In tagmemic theory, each unit of the phonological hierarchy has three modes; the feature mode, the manifestation mode, the distribution mode. (A good, understandable, two-page summary of tagmemic theory is given in K. Pike, 1973.)

8.1.1. *The feature mode*

The feature mode (294-306, 365-77, 392-97) consists of the contrastive-identificational features. It is these features which differentiate every unit from every other unit that is on the same level of the phonological system of which it is a part. That is, it is the contrastive-identificational features that cause one unit to be in contrast with other units. It is also the contrastive-identificational features which permit the unit to be identified even when, in some environments, it may not be in contrast with all the other units.

A unit has both a nucleus and margins. On the phoneme level (308), the nucleus may be either at the point of the greatest degree of closure, or the greatest degree of opening. On the syllable level (372), the nucleus is the syllabic part of the syllable, but may include nonsyllabic elements. (For example the nucleus may include a glottal stop.) On the word or phrase level (395), the nucleus would be the stressed syllable, or it may include more than one stressed syllable if the nucleus is complex. Other units, for example the syllable (371-72), and the phoneme (317) may also have complex nuclei.

The margins of a unit may also be contrastive-identificational features. That is, the approach (the on-glide) to a nucleus, or the release (the off-glide) of a nucleus may be contrastive (308, 370-71, 396). For a discussion of the etics of a rhythm wave with its nucleus and margins, see (545-50 and also K. Pike, 1962).

Because of symmetry and distribution within the system, a nucleus which is etically simple, may consist of two units. For example, in some languages, a long vocoid may be two emic syllables (380, 549), and a nasalized vocoid may be emically vowel plus nasal consonant (317, 548).

8.1.2. *The manifestation mode*

The manifestation mode of a unit (306-18, 377-84, 397-99) is made up of its variants, its allophones. A unit is primarily a unit of behavior, the activity of an individual, and the movement of the body parts involved. Such movements are not physical absolutes; they are not constants, rather they are relative to the movements of other units with which they are in contrast. Units may change in relation to their environments. They are identifiable in each environment in relation to the other units which occur in that specific environment. The variant which occurs most frequently, and which is less affected by its environments, is called the "norm" (313).

8.1.3. *The distribution mode*

The distribution mode of a unit (318-22, 384-91, 399-402) is its potential for occurrence in some slot or slots within a larger unit, its potential for occurrence in a sequence or in a system. For example, some phonemes in a certain language may precede the vowel within a syllable, but never follow it. Or, some syllables may occur in the nucleus of the phonological word (that is, stressed), but do not occur in the margin (that is, nonstressed). Or, some phonemes, in a certain language, although they may occur final in a syllable, never occur final in a pause group. Or, some consonants (but not all) may precede certain other consonants in a specific language.

A further component of a phonological unit is its distribution within the lexical or grammatical hierarchies. The distribution of some phonemes, for example, may be restricted to stem versus clitic (312). The distribution of the nucleus of a stress group may be restricted to the first syllable of the stem (385).

The distribution of a unit is important in the identification of that unit. For example, [i] is /i/ when in the syllable nucleus, but /y/ when in the syllable margin; [A] may be an allophone of /a/ in some environments, but an allophone of the consonant /h/ in other environments.

In a sequence of units, there may be an indeterminacy of the distribution of the unit which occurs at the border between units of a higher level. It may be indeterminate with respect to its occurrence at the end of the first unit versus at the beginning of the second. In some instances, the unit of the lower level may actually be in double function (381-82). That is, it is simultaneously a member of both larger units. For example, the phoneme /d/ in *bedding* may be a member of both the first and the second syllables. Also when a syllable occurs at the end of one stress group at the same time it is the beginning of the next, it is a syllable in double function (385).

8.2. *Other books on tagmemic phonology*

Crawford in his *Totontepec Mixe phonotagmemics* (1963) sets up a

76

phonotagmeme. The phonotagmeme is the correlation between the class of phonemes which may occur in the slot of a syllable (or in the slot of some other higher-level unit) and the slot itself. Then there is a correlation between the class of syllables which may occur in the slot of a higher-level unit and the slot itself. He has a phonological hierarchy of phonotagmemic units which is in addition to the phonological hierarchy described by K. Pike. For a discussion of the difference between his hierarchies and that of K. Pike, see Crawford, 1963:166-88, and also K. Pike, 1967:520.

8.3. Grimes' Phonological Analysis, Part I

The first impression of Grimes' textbook on phonological analysis (1969) is that its basic theory is very different from that found in K. Pike's *Phonemics* (1947) and *Language* (1967). On closer study, however, it becomes apparent that much of the difference is one of terminology. He has avoided the use of many of the older terms. For example, instead of "contrast", he used "discrimination" (89-120); instead of "symmetry", he uses "homomorphic" (95, 146-49); instead of "interpretation procedures", he uses "resegmentation" (58, 70-88); instead of "suspect", he uses "ambivalent" (77-80). He emphasizes the use of frames to determine the segments that have to be distinguished (41-63, 90). He also emphasizes a "matching" technique (141-55) whereby the segments in one slot are compared with the segments in another slot. Perhaps he hopes that by using the frame and matching techniques, the need for "phonetic similarity" (129-31) as a tool in phonological analysis will be lessened.

8.4. Bee's Neo-Tagmemics

In her textbook *Neo-Tagmemics*, Bee (1973) has given a clearly written summary of the tagmemic theory of the phoneme. She has also included a little about levels higher than the phoneme. Throughout the book she has emphasized that the same analytical procedures can be applied to all three hierarchies. She, for the most part, refers the student to the Robinson's *workbook* (1970) for exercises. More recently, I have published (1975) a workbook which includes higher level phonological problems.

Sivertsen (1960) uses the phonological hierarchy in her analysis of one dialect of English.

REFERENCES

Abrahamson, Arne
1968   "Contrastive distribution of phoneme classes in Içua Tupi", *Anthropological Linguistics* 10, 6:11-21.

Allen, Janice Dodson and Phyllis Walker Hurd
  1972   "Manambu phonemes", *Te Reo* 15, 37-44.
Aschmann, Herman P.
  1946   "Totonaco phonemes", *International Journal of American Linguistics* 12, 34-43.
Bauernschmidt, Amy
  1965   "Amuzgo syllable dynamics", *Language* 41, 471-83.
Beasley, David and Kenneth L. Pike
  1957   "Notes on Huambisa phonemics", *Lingua* 6, 1-8.
Bee, Darlene L.
  1973   *Neo-Tagmemics, An integrated approach to linguistic analysis and description*, ed. by Alan Healey and Doreen Marks (Ukarumpa, Papua New Guinea: Summer Institute of Linguistics).
Bendor-Samuel, John T.
  1960   "Some problems of segmentation in the phonological analysis of Tereno", *Word* 16, 348-55.
  1963   "Stress in Terena", *Transactions of the Philological Scoeity for 1962* (Oxford), 105-23.
Bloch, Bernard
  1941   "Phonemic overlapping", *American Speech* 16, 278-84.
Blood, David L.
  1967   "Phonological units in Cham", *Anthropological Linguistics* 9, 8.15-32.
Brichoux, Robert
  1970   "Sindangan Subamun phonemics", *Papers in Philippine Linguistics*, 3 (= *Pacific Linguistics*, series A, 24) Canberra: Australian National University), 71-77.
Bridgeman, Loraine I.
  1961   "Kaiwa (Guarani) phonology", *International Journal of American Linguistics* 27, 329-32.
Bunn, Gordon and Ruth
  1970   "Golin phonology", *Papers in New Guinea Linguistics* (=*Pacific Linguistics*, series A, 23) Canberra: Australian National University), 1-6.
Burgess, Don H.
  1970   "Tarahumara phonology (Rocoroibo Dialect)", *Studies in Language and Linguistics, 1969-70*, ed. by Ralph W. Ewton, Jr. and Jacob Ornstein (El Paso: Texas Western Press), 45-65.
Burgess, Eunice and Patricia Ham
  1968   "Multilevel conditioning of phoneme variants in Apinayé", *Linguistics* 41, 5-18.
Caughley, Ross
  1970   "Pitch, intensity, and higher levels in Chepang", *Studies on tone and phonological segments* (= *Tone systems of Tibeto-Burman languages of Nepal*, 1), ed. by Austin Hale and Kenneth L. Pike (Urbana: University of Illinois), 143-57.
Cooper, James and Nancy
  1966   "Halang phonemes", *Mon-Khmer Studies II*, (= *Linguistic Circle of Saigon Publication*, 3) ed. by David Thomas, Nguyễn Dình Hòa and David Blood (Saigon: Linguistic Circle of Saigon and Summer Institute of Linguistics), 87-98.
Crawford, John Chapman
  1963   *Totontepec Mixe phonotagmemics* (= Summer Institute of Linguistics Publications in Linguistics and Related Fields, 8) (Norman, Oklahoma: Summer Institute of Linguistics of the University of Oklahoma).

78

Delattre, Pierre
1964   "German phonetics between English and French", *Linguistics* 8, 43-55.
Denes, Peter B. and Elliot N. Pinson
1963   *The speech chain* (Baltimore: Waverly Press).
Elson, Ben
1947   "Sierra Popoluca syllable structure", *International Journal of American Linguistics* 13, 13-17.
Engel, Ralph and Robert E. Longacre
1963   "Syntactic matrices in Ostuacan Zoque", *International Journal of American Linguistics* 29, 331-44.
Foris, David
1973   "Sochiapan Chinantec syllable structure", *International Journal of American Linguistics* 39, 232-35.
Franklin, Joyce
1965   "Kewa II: Higher level phonology", *Anthropological Linguistics* 7, 5:84-88.
Gibson, Lorna F.
1956   "Pame (Otomi) phonemics and morphophonemics", *International Journal of American Linguistics* 22, 242-65.
Glover, Warren W.
1969   *Gurung phonemic summary* (= *Tibeto-Burman phonemic summaries*) (Kirtipur: SIL and Tribhuvan University).
Gordon, Kent
1970   "Sherpa tone and higher levels", *Studies on tone and phonological segments* (= *Tone systems of Tibeto-Burman languages of Nepal,* 1), ed. by Austin Hale and Kenneth L. Pike (Urbana: University of Illinois), 186-206.
Grimes, Joseph E.
1959   "Huichol tone and intonation", *International Journal of American Linguistics* 25, 221-32.
1969   *Phonological analysis, Part I* (Santa Ana, California: Summer Institute of Linguistics).
Hari, Maria, Doreen Taylor, and Kenneth L. Pike
1970   "Tamang tone and higher levels", *Studies on tone and phonological segments* (= *Tone systems of Tibeto-Burman languages of Nepal,* 1), ed. by Austin Hale and Kenneth L. Pike (Urbana: University of Illinois), 82-124.
Harris, Zellig S.
1951   *Methods in structural linguistics* (Chicago: The University of Chicago Press).
Harrison, Carl H. and John M. Taylor
1971   "Nasalization in Kaiwá", *Tupi studies, I* (= *Summer Institute of Linguistics Publications in Linguistics and Related Fields*, 29) (Norman, Oklahoma: Summer Institute of Linguistics of the University of Oklahoma), 15-20.
Haupers, Ralph
1969   "Stieng phonemes", *Mon-Khmer studies III* (= *Linguistic Circle of Saigon Publication*, 4), 131-37.
Hoard, J.E.
1966   "Juncture and syllable structure in English", *Phonetica* 15, 96-109.
Hockett, Charles F.
1955   *A manual of phonology* (= *Indiana University Publications in Anthropology and Linguistics*, memoir 11), *International Journal of American Linguistics* 21:4 (Part 1).
Hudson, Joyce and Eirlys Richards
1969   "The phonology of Walmatjari", *Oceanic Linguistics* 8, 2.171-89.

Hunter, Georgia G. and Eunice V. Pike
   1969   "The phonology and tone sandhi of Molinos Mixtec", *Linguistics* 47,
             24-40.
Johnson, Orville E. and Catherine Peeke
   1962   "Phonemic units in the Secoya word", *Studies in Ecuadorian Indian
             languages,* I (= *SIL Publications in Linguistics and Related Fields,* 7)
             (Norman, Oklahoma: Summer Institute of Linguistics of the University of
             Oklahoma), 78-95.
Kalstrom, Marjorie R. and Eunice V. Pike
   1968   "Stress in the phonological system of Eastern Popoloca", *Phonetica* 18,
             16-30.
Larsen, Raymond S. and Eunice V. Pike
   1949   "Huasteco intonations and phonemes", *Language* 25, 268-77.
Lehiste, Ilse
   1960   *An acoustic-phonetic study of internal open juncture. Phonetica* 5,
             Supplement.
   1964   *Acoustical characteristics of selected English consonants* (= *Indiana
             University Research Center in Anthropology, Folklore, and Linguistics,*
             publication 34) (Bloomington: Indiana University).
   1970   *Suprasegmentals* (Cambridge, Mass.: M.I.T. Press).
Liccardi, Millicent and Joseph Grimes
   1968   "Itonama intonation and phonemes", *Linguistics* 38, 36-41.
Lloyd, J. and A. Healey
   1970   "Barua phonemes: A problem in interpretation", *Linguistics* 60, 33-48.
Longacre, Robert E.
   1952   "Five phonemic pitch levels in Trique", *Acta Linguistica* 7, 62-82.
Loving, Richard
   1966   "Awa phonemes, tonemes, and tonally differentiated allomorphs", *Papers
             in New Guinea Linguistics,* 5 (= *Linguistic Circle of Canberra Publications,*
             series A, 7) (Canberra: Australian National University), 23-32. Republished
             in *The languages of the Estern family of the East New Guinea Highland
             stock,* ed. by Howard McKaughan (Seattle: University of Washington,
             1973, 10-18.
Malécot, André
   1963   "Luiseño. A structural analysis I: Phonology", *International Journal of
             American Linguistics* 29, 89-95.
Marsh, James
   1969   "Mantjiltjara phonology", *Oceanic Linguistics* 8, 2.131-52.
Maryott, Kenneth R.
   1961   "The phonology and morphophonemics of Tabukang Sangir", *Philippine
             Social Sciences and Humanities Review* 26, 111-26.
May, Jean and Eunice Loeweke
   1965   "The phonological hierarchy in Fasu", *Anthropological Linguistics* 7,
             5:89-97.
McElhanon, K.A.
   1970   *Selepet phonology* (= *Pacific Linguistics,* series B,14) (Canberra: The
             Australian National University).
McMahon, Ambrose
   1967   "Phonemes and phonemic units of Cora (Mexico)", *International Journal
             of American Linguistics* 33, 128-34.
Merrifield, William R.
   1963   "Palantla Chinantec syllable types", *Anthropological Linguistics* 5, 5:1-16.
Migliazza, Ernest and Joseph E. Grimes
   1961   "Shiriana phonology", *Anthropological Linguistics* 3, 6:31-41.

80

Minor, Eugene E.
1956   "Witoto vowel clusters", *International Journal of American Linguistics* 22, 131-37.
Morse, Robert H.
1963   "Phonology of Rawang", *Anthropological Linguistics* 5, 5:17-41.
Moser, Edward and Mary B. Moser
1965   "Consonant vowel balance in Seri (Hokan) syllables", *Linguistics* 16, 50-67.
Murane, John and Elizabeth
1972   "Vocalic syllabicity in Daga", *Phonetica* 25, 19-26.
Nasr, Raja T.
1964   "Phonemic velarization in literacy Arabic", *Proceedings of the 9th International Congress of Linguists, Cambridge, Mass. Aug. 27-31, 1962,* ed. by Horace G. Lunt (=*Janua Linguarum*, series maior, 12) (The Hague: Mouton), 453-55.
Newell, Leonard E.
1970   "Phonology of Batad Ifugao", *Philippine Journal of Linguistics* 1, 1:101-17.
Newman, Stanley
1947   "Bella Coola I: Phonology", *International Journal of American Linguistics* 13.129-34.
Olson, Ronald D.
1967   "The syllable in Chipaya", *International Journal of American Linguistics* 33,300-04.
Orr, Carolyn
1962   "Ecuador Quichua phonology", *Studies in Ecuadorian Indian Languages: I* (=*SIL Publications in Linguistics and Related Fields*, 7) (Norman, Oklahoma: Summer Institute of Linguistics of the University of Oklahoma), 60-77.
Osborn, Henry A. Jr.
1966   "Warao I: Phonology and morphophonemics", *International Journal of American Linguistics* 32.108-23.
Pankratz, Leo and Eunice V. Pike
1967   "Phonology and morphotonemics of Ayutla Mixtec", *International Journal of American Linguistics* 33, 287-99.
Pence, Alan
1964   "Intonation in Kunimaipa", *Papers in New Guinea Linguistics*, 1 (= *Linguistic Circle of Canberra Publications* series A, 3) (Canberra: Australian National University), 1-15.
Pike, Eunice V.
1948   "Problems in Zapotec tone analysis", *International Journal of American Linguistics* 14, 161-70. Reprinted in *Studies in Tone and Intonation* ed. by Ruth M. Brend (= Biblioteca Phonetica, no. 11; Basel: S. Karger) 1975, 84-99.
1951   "Tonemic-intonemic correlation in Mazahua (Otomi)", *International Journal of American Linguistics* 17, 37-41.
1964   "The phonology of New Guinea Highlands languages", *New Guinea: The Central Highlands*, ed. by James B. Watson (=*American Anthropologist*, 66:4, part 2), 121-32.
1967   "Huautla de Jiménez Mazatec", *Handbook of Middle American Indians* Volume 5, *Linguistics* ed. Norman A. McQuown, (Austin: University of Texas Press) 311-30.
1974   *Advanced phonology workbook: a hierarchical approach* (including both student's and instructor's copy) (Norman, Oklahoma: Summer Institute of Linguistics).

81

Pike, Eunice V. and Eugene Scott
1962   "The phonological hierarchy of Marinahua", *Phonetica* 8, 1-8. Reprinted in Studies in Tone and Intonation ed. by Ruth M. Brend
(= Bibliotheca Phonetica, no. 11) Basel: S. Karger 1975; 196-203.

Pike, Eunice V. and Priscilla Small
1973   "Downstepping terrace tone in Coatzospan Mixtec", *Advances in
Tagmemics*, ed. by Ruth M. Brend (Amsterdam: North-Holland Publishing
Company), 105-34.

Pike, Kenneth L.
1945   *The intonation of American English* (= University of Michigan Publications, Linguistics 1) (Ann Arbor: University of Michigan Press).
1947   *Phonemics: A technique for reducing languages to writing* (= University of
Michigan Publications, Linguistics, 3) (Ann Arbor: University of Michigan
Press).
1957   "Abdominal pulse types in some Peruvian languages", *Language* 33, 30-35.
1959   "Language as particle, wave, and field", *The Texas Quarterly* 2, 2.37-54.
Reprinted in *Kenneth L. Pike: Selected Writings*, ed. by Ruth M. Brend
(The Hague: Mouton), 1972, 129-43.
1962   "Practical phonetics of rhythm waves", *Phonetica* 8, 9-30.
1967   *Language in relation to a unified theory of the structure of human
behavior*, 2nd edition (The Hague: Mouton).
1970   "The role of nuclei of feet in the analysis of tone in Tibeto-Burman
languages of Nepal", *Prosodic feature analysis/Analyse des faits
prosodiques*, ed. by Léon, Faure, and Rigault (Montreal: Librairie Didier),
153-64.
1973   "Science fiction as a test of axioms concerning human behavior", *Parma
Eldalamberon* 1.3.

Pike, Kenneth L. and Eunice V. Pike
1947   "Immediate constituents of Mazateco syllables", *International Journal of
American Linguistics* 13, 78-91.

Pike, Kenneth L. and Willard Kindberg
1956   "A problem in multiple stresses", *Word* 12, 415-28.

Powlison, Esther
1971   "The suprahierarchical and hierarchical structures of Yagua phonology",
Linguistics 75, 43-73.

Priest, Perry
1968   "Phonemes of the Sirionó language", *Linguistics* 41, 102-08.

Ray, Punya Sloka
1967   "Dafla phonology and morphology", *Anthropological Linguistics* 9,
8:9-14.

Reid, Lawrence A.
1963   "Phonology of central Bontoc", *Journal of the Polynesian Society* 72,
1:21-26.

Rensch, Calvin R. and Carolyn M.
1966   "The Lalana Chinantec syllable", *Summa Anthropologica en homenaje a
Roberto J. Weitlaner* (Mexico: Instituto Nacional de Antropologia e
Historia), 455-63.

Rich, Furne
1963   "Arabela phonemes and high-level phonology", *Studies in Peruvian Indian
languages* 1 (= *Summer Institute of Linguistics Publications in Linguistics
and Related Fields* 9) (Norman, Oklahoma: Summer Institute of
Linguistics of the University of Oklahoma), 193-206.

Robbins, Frank E.
1961   "Quiotepec Chinantec syllable patterning", *International Journal of*

82

          American Linguistics 27, 237-50.
1968   *Quiotepec Chinantec grammar* (=*Papeles de la Chinantla* IV, Serie
          Científica, 8) Mexico: Museo Nacional de Anthropología).
Robinson, Dow F.
1970   *Workbook for phonological analysis* (Santa Ana, California: Summer
          Institute of Linguistics).

Romeo, Luigi
1964   "Toward a phonological grammar of modern spoken Greek", *Special
          Publication*, 5 (= *Word* 20:3), 60-78.

Saxton, Dean
1963   "Papago phonemes", *International Journal of American Linguistics* 29,
          29-35.

Siertsema, B.
1959   "Stress and tone in Yoruba word composition", *Lingua* 8, 385-402.
Sinclair, Donald E. and Kenneth L. Pike
1948   "The tonemes of Mesquital Otomo", *International Journal of American
          Linguistics* 14, 91-98.

Sivertsen, Eva
1960   *Cockney phonology* (Oslo University Press).

Skinner, Leo E.
1962   "Usila·Chinantec syllable structure", *International Journal of American
          Linguistics* 28, 251-55.

Smalley, William A.
1953   "Phonemic rhythm in Comanche", *International Journal of American
          Linguistics* 19, 297-301.

Smith, Kenneth D.
1968   "Laryngealization and de-laryngealization in Sedang phonemics",
          Linguistics 38, 52-69.

Solomon, Zomaya S. and Robert K. Headley, Jr.
1973   "The phonology of modern spoken Syriac", *Anthropological Linguistics*
          15.3.136-47.

Sommer, B.A.
1969   *Kunjen Phonology: Synchronic and diachronic* (=*Pacific Linguistics*, series
          B, 11) (Canberra: Australian National University).

Steinkraus, Walter
1969   "Tifal phonology showing vowel and tone neutralization", *Kivung* 2,
          57-66.

Stringer, Mary and Joyce Hotz
1971   "Waffa phonemes", *Te Reo* 14, 42-48.

Swick, Joyce
1966   "Chuave phonological hierarchy", *Papers in New Guinea Linguistics*, 5 (=
          Linguistic Circle of Canberra Publications, series A, 7) (Canberra:
          Australian National University), 33-48.

Trammell, Robert L.
1971   "The phonology of the northern standard dialect of Bhojpuri", *Anthropo-
          logical Linguistics* 13, 4:126-41.

Turner, Paul
1967   "Highland Chontal phonemics", *Anthropological Linguistics* 9, 4:26-32.
West, John David
1962   "The phonology of Mikasuki", *Studies in Linguistics* 16, 3-4:77-91.
Westley, David O.
1971   "The Tepetotutla Chinantec stressed syllable", *International Journal of
          American Linguistics* 37, 160-63.

Wheeler, Alva and Margaret
    1962   "Siona phonemics (Western Tucanoan)", *Studies in Ecuadorian Indian languages:* I (= *SIL Publications in Linguistics and Related Fields, 7)* (Norman, Oklahoma: Summer Institute of Linguistics of the University of Oklahoma), 96-111.
Williams, Ann F. and Eunice V. Pike
    1968   "The phonology of Western Popoloca", *Lingua* 20, 368-80.
Yotsukura, Sayo
    1967   "The Japanese tone and intonation systems", *Linguistics* 35, 66-105.

LANGUAGE AND BEHAVIOR

MARY RUTH WISE

Summer Institute of Linguistics

"The really revolutionary concept that Pike presents in his book [*Language in Relation to a Unified Theory of the structure of Human Behavior*] is that all human behavior is structured in a similar way or in the same way" (Bee, 1973:v).

Pike himself, in commenting on tagmemics and the scope of his own theoretical interests, says:

I'm interested in truth about man, about how language is related to man, about how language is related to behavior. I wouldn't ever grant that I'm interested only in language (P. Fries, 1972:195 quoting discussion following Pike, 1971:162).

P. Fries, as well as Bee, believes that this breadth of focus is perhaps the most important distinguishing characteristic of tagmemic theory. It is this breadth of focus — language *and* behavior — which constitutes the subject matter for this chapter.

Many of the topics discussed in this paper are beginning to receive attention from those working within other theories, and the facts will no doubt be accounted for differently than they would be within tagmemics. What is especially distinctive to tagmemics is that, as a consequence of its breadth of focus, these questions were anticipated in Pike's work a decade or more before other theoreticians turned their attention to them.

These topics include: 1) Case or roles of arguments in underlying structure — seen in Pike's "actor-as-subject versus recipient-of-action as subject" (1954:131).[1] 2) Speaker viewpoint (including topics such as topicalization, contrast, etc.) — seen in Pike's portmanteau tagmemes of subject-focus-emphasis (1963b). 3) Social context of language (including related topics such as appropriateness of an utterance and presuppositions) — seen in Pike's postulating that language units are distributed "within similarly organized but larger units, units of a nonlanguage type" (1954:6-7). In a more explicit statement he says: "Communication requires understanding, and understanding requires a ... pool of common experience, or field, against which particular speech events at a particular moment stand out as figure on ground ... (1959:51).

In contrast, the importance of context was explicitly rejected in 1963 in an important article on transformational grammar:

Grammars seek to describe the structure of a sentence *in isolation from its possible settings in linguistic discourse (written or verbal) or in non-linguistic contexts (social or physical* ... [since] the fluent speaker is able to construct and recognize syntactically well-formed sentences without recourse to information about settings (Katz and Fodor, 1963:484).

A changing trend, however, is seen in a recent article by R. Lakoff. She acknowledges specifically that Pike, as well as many from other schools of thought, anticipated that:

Contextual factors, social and otherwise, must be taken into account in determining the acceptability and interpretation of sentences ... Contextual factors cannot be avoided by the linguist of any theoretical view, if he is to deal honestly and accurately with the facts of language (1972:926, fn. 12).[2]

Besides emphasizing that language must be considered in its social context, tagmemics holds as a basic assumption that language, and human behavior in general, is purposeful or meaningful.[3] Furthermore, "every purposeful activity of man is structured, and ... certain basic characteristics are common to every such activity, so that it should be possible to develop a theory and a technique which would pass without jar from the study of the structure of one kind of activity of man to that of any other kind" (Pike, 1956:59). Thus, both verbal and nonverbal behavior are treated within a single unified theory in which human behavior is "analyzed as consisting of various simultaneous structurings [i.e., modes] of its activity" (Pike, 1967:93).

In section 1, verbal and nonverbal behavior are discussed with reference to these modes, especially with regard to the inextricable fusion of verbal and nonverbal behavior in the manifestation mode and with regard to language in its sociocultural setting in the distribution mode. In section 2, language functions and meaning are discussed, especially in relation to the observer, and "situational roles" in sociocultural meaning. Interrelations between various components of meaning and functions of language are also discussed. In section 1, the reader will note that the theoretical viewpoint has remained basically the same since the inception of tagmemics and that recent studies further expand and illustrate the concepts discussed with little theoretical development. On the other hand, there has been more development and alternative views have been proposed regarding meaning and role, as seen in section 2.

1. TRIMODAL STRUCTURE OF VERBAL AND
NONVERBAL BEHAVIOR

"A *behavioreme* [a unit of behavior] is an emic segment or component of purposive human activity, hierarchically and trimodally structured..." (*Ibid.*: 121). The feature mode, the manifestation mode, and the distribution mode comprise the three simultaneous structurings of human behavior.

1.1. *The feature mode*

Simultaneously occurring contrastive-identificational features comprise the feature mode of an emic unit of behavior. Discussion in this section will be primarily on features in relation to meaning and purpose. "One of the observable elements of human behavior... is precisely the fact that participants in that behavior affirm an awareness or knowledge of meaning or purpose" (*Ibid.*:156).

1.1.1. *Emic and etic viewpoints*

Meaning and purpose are closely linked to the basic tagmemic concepts of the role of the observer in the study of human behavior and the contrast between etic and emic viewpoints. In tagmemics one is interested in accounting for "behavior *as people react to it*, i.e., in reference to its emic structuring ... [so that] choice and purpose must be included" (*Ibid.*:197). The identificational-contrastive features of a unit are part of the emic view, while variations, such as those illustrated in the following, are etic: "Tagmemic theory staked its claims on the belief that essential to the description of human behavior as we live it must be the ability to recognize a friend even though he has just had Wheaties for breakfast, cut his long hair, and replaced his necktie" (Pike, 1971:80).

Another characteristic difference between emic and etic viewpoints is that the latter is cross-cultural while the former is relevant within a specific system. Thus, the observationally identical may be systematically different while the observationally different may be systematically the same. "Etic criteria are frequently ... measurable as such, without reference to the system in which they are embedded, while emic criteria are contrastive, and observable in reference to differential response which they elicit in relation to other units of the system" (Pike, 1957:38). Consider, for example, raising the voice in Amuesha and Aguaruna:

Anger is the worst moral offense to the Amuesha, and since raising the voice signifies anger to them, they usually speak in a quiet, low manner. Shouting is acceptable only in calling to someone at a distance; unacceptable shouting, of course, occurs in spite of the sanctions against it. The reaction of the Amuesha to the Aguaruna, who speak in a very loud manner, ... [is as] one Amuesha commented: "Those Aguarunas speak as though they are angry all the time." The Aguaruna, on the other hand, [who practice revenge-killing and, therefore, announce their arrival noisily, if they've come peaceably] react in the opposite way: "The man who is quiet is probably doing something bad" (Wise, 1971:23).

Hymes notes that "Pike's conceptual distinction, *emic : etic,* has become a standard, if much debated, part of general anthropology" (1969:361). However, since most of the anthropological studies utilizing this concept are not otherwise within the tagmemic framework, they will not be treated in this paper. (For extensive discussion of etic and emic contrasts in grammar, see especially the work of Longacre, e.g., 1964.)

1.1.2. *The role of the observer and native reaction*

The role of the observer is crucial in arriving at an emic understanding of behavior. "The observer 'understands' an event, principle, or situation only when it appears to fit into his larger experience as a special instance of kinds of relationships which he has elsewhere learned and built unconsciously into a structured frame of reference, which sets up the basis for him to react to relationships in general" (Pike, 1965:286).

The detached observer, as a non-participant in a culture, tends to view things and events etically, and *"the observer adds part of himself to the data* that he looks at or listens to" (Pike, 1964c:129). On the other hand, the observer who is involved as a participant in a culture sees the internal relations and purpose of an event. Consequently, if the anthropologist or linguist, as an outside observer, "is to study behavior *as it actually functions,* ... [he must assume that he] can detect the presence and to some degree the nature of meaning and purpose" (Pike, 1967:158). Although he recognizes that the members of a society are often unable to state verbally what is emic in their behavior and are, in fact, often unconscious of the abstract system, the field worker, nevertheless, assumes that the verbalized purposes of a community are highly relevant to the activity of that community and that they may be emic abstractions from various contexts (Pike, 1955).

Thus, the study of native reaction is seen as an important aspect of any study of human behavior, and is itself a kind of verbal behavior. In such a study "it is important to note clearly the difference between an appeal to a 'feeling' which is inaccessible to direct observation, as over against observable, testable, independently verifiable abilities or objective responses of language speakers" (Pike, 1967:67).

Pike also points out that native participants "(in many instances at least) react to that behavior as if it were composed of discrete particles" (1956:661). That is, they react to units, having closure signalled by overt, objective cultural cues, as in the Nomatsiguenga case where an informant considered a certain taped recording of a story as somehow incomplete and asked "didn't he say 'that's all'? " (Wise, 1971:157).

Grimes, in discussing discourse structure, begins with Pike's concepts:

> Chunks of human behavior exist and ... are recognizable to those who participate in them, and often to bystanders who understand the cultural systems involved, as having a definite beginning and end. Behavior that is characterized thus by closure is Pike's starting point for the analysis of both verbal and nonverbal behavior (1972:26).

With regard to verbal behavior, the need for carefully controlled psycholinguistic experiments in order to safely base linguistic theory on a functional view of language is commented on by Pike (1958a:588). However, not many such experiments within the tagmemic framework have been reported. In one of the few, Gudschinsky and the Popoviches give psycholinguistic evidence to support an analysis of Maxakalí phonology in which certain syllabic vocoids are considered to be allophones of consonant phonemes. They hesitated to offer such an analysis on the basis of distributional and phonetic criteria alone, but in the tagmemic model "it is assumed that the units of a language are psychologically real to naïve native speakers, and that this psychological reality can be demonstrated by observable behavior" (1970:87). They, therefore, did extensive testing with one informant who was far from functionally literate — training him to read words, and to build them from dictation, using Maxakalí letters having approximately the same values they have in Portuguese. In later stages they asked him to build words which included the syllabic allophones of consonants. He invariably chose consonant symbols to represent the syllabic allophones. In a subsequent literacy project, naïve monolinguals learned to read easily and "some Maxakalí, already familiar with the letters of Portuguese, learned to read their own language with a few hours of instruction" (*Ibid.*).

In a different area of language structure, an experiment was conducted to test the ability of college students who were native speakers of English to identify paragraph boundaries in both English and nonsense passages. The students were able to verbalize reactions to various systems, but "it appears that formal cues are more important than semantic ones in the task of recognizing paragraph structure" (Koen, Becker, and Young, 1968:187).

In Nomatsiguenga Campa the reaction of an illiterate informant also seems to confirm the psychological reality of units beyond the sentence. After discussion the informant pointed out places where the story 'changes a little'. The breaks he indicated are remarkably close to those I would posit as grammatical, i.e., surface-structure, paragraph boundaries rather than deep structure boundaries. His reactions thus parallel those of the college students mentioned above. (For details of this experiment, see Wise, 1971:8-9, 203-205).

In an attempt to arrive at the native model of certain spatial concepts, Sarles, building on Pike's suggestion, assumed that:

> Language and interactional-communication behavior (which seem to be more intimately related than modern linguistics would admit) have a formal relationship in question-answer, interactional settings. That is, the answer or response to particular questions appears to be a formal (rule regulated), 'shared' system (Sarles, 1970:79).

The relationship between questions and responses and the classes of responses are studied in terms of their membership, variations, and culturally relevant characteristics. The linguist-anthropologist "attempts to allow the native speaker to categorize reality in his native world, preserving the contexts, while the [outside] observer manipulates some formally discoverable and describable part of language to show up [the relevant categories]" (*Ibid*.:81).

Sarles examined classes and sub-classes of questions and found that the Tzotzil world is divided into two parts (near and far) and that distance is relative to the kind of action. During the study, the analyst allowed the informant to give him the essential context of the response and arrange the elements into classes according to the native model. "By beginning with a culturally occurring situation, using grammar to isolate elements, and concentrating on a two-person scheme, the observer is enabled to make statements concerning some other cultural universe" (*Ibid*.:100). (Cf. section 2.2. for further discussion of Sarles' work.)

The works cited in the preceding paragraphs are some of the principal ones on native reaction and the role of the observer in studying human behavior. (In section 2.1. the observer as speaker, i.e., an active participant in verbal behavior, is discussed.) It is hoped that further development of these concepts, which are basic to tagmemic theory, will become a growing trend.

1.2. The manifestation mode

Actually occurring verbal and nonverbal actions comprise the manifestation mode of units of behavior. Tagmemics thus rejects rigid distinctions between *la langue: la parole*, competence: performance, and content:expression with their resultant view of language as a series of abstract mappings from meaning to sound. A study of language in the abstract is considered useful and interesting for certain purposes, but an overly compartmentalized framework is rejected. Tagmemics is a theory of language as speech in relation to other forms of human behavior. Pike comments on the *langue: parole* compartmentalization as follows:

> As more and more materials in speech [voice quality, etc.] begin to appear structured, the view that 'language' as a structure differs from 'speech' as activity is threatened ... Furthermore, the structural units always retain substance as relevant to their manifestation mode (1967:536).[4]

Although he does not adopt the tagmemic model, Searle, in an essay on the philosophy of language, also takes the view that a study of language in the abstract is not adequate:

> A theory of language is part of a theory of action, simply because speaking is a rule-governed form of behavior ... A great deal can be said in the study of language without studying speech acts, but any such purely formal theory is necessarily incomplete (1969:17).

(It should perhaps be emphasized here that although a great deal is said within tagmemics about verbal and nonverbal behavior, it is not a behavioristic theory. Observed forms are only part of inseparable form-meaning composites. Moreover, observed behavior is only one mode of language and other cultural units: the manifestation mode. The feature mode, including meaning and purpose, and the distribution mode are equally important.)

Consideration of the manifestation mode of language makes it imperative that language and other behavior be treated as an integrated whole. Pike supports this view "by showing (1) that language behavior and nonlanguage behavior are fused in single events, and (2) that verbal and nonverbal elements may at times substitute structurally for one another in function" (1967:26). His illustrations of the latter include greetings, grimaces and exclamations substituting for each other, etc. The former is illustrated by a recording of breakfast table conversation and accompanying actions, and by nonlanguage reports and actions such as a baptismal service which needs the accompanying verbal formula (*Ibid.*:25-36, 73-97). Party games in which, on each repetition of a song, gestures are progressively substituted for words in a single emic unit of activity provide another example of fusion of verbal and nonverbal behavior (Pike, 1956:668).

In a slightly different kind of example, Barnwell states that in conversation the linguistic and nonlinguistic contexts are more closely interrelated than in narration and that, consequently, the object in Mbembe is quite commonly implicit in the nonlinguistic context (1966:162).

Gudschinsky (1968) describes the verbal and nonverbal components of several behavioral units of five indigenous tribes of Brazil. Her analysis does not give complete descriptions of the language and sociocultural systems, but it is sufficiently detailed so that the reader sees clearly that certain nonverbal acts would be incomplete without the culturally expected accompanying phrases; the converse is also true: certain verbal expressions need to be accompanied by nonverbal acts. It is further shown that in some cases verbal and nonverbal behavior can be substituted for one another within socially acceptable norms.

Dressler (1970) also includes reference to verbal-nonverbal relationships, especially in showing relations between speech context and speech formulation. Although his emphasis is primarily on the development of a text-syntax model, he does comment that the preferred model is the one closer to observable speech reality.

Turning to a very practical application of the concept, the interpenetration of verbal and nonverbal behavior is strikingly seen in language learning. In speaking of the crystallization or nucleation of structures in the learner's mind, Pike reminds the student:

Language is more than organized verbal sound. It is a part of life's total behavioral action and structure ... Greeting forms in a classroom situation, simulated market scenes, and the like, provide the larger structural niches within which added bits of learning fit.

Nucleation here is not at all dependent upon the *extent* of the vocabulary which he has mastered, nor accuracy, but upon the capacity to use a small set of forms in a natural way automatically in a natural context (1960a:292-293).

The interpenetration of verbal and nonverbal behavior is even more strikingly seen in monolingual language learning situations. Pike affirms:

There must be a physical matrix within which the language events occur. There must be at least two men present, providing a simple social structure ... These men must be assumed to have the normal capacities of men to recognize relationships, proportions, and analogies, under gestural conditions. There must be observable actions and re-actions (1958b:385).

Gesture is important also as it intersects with vocal systems: This intersection enables one to recognize and differentiate emotional states. In Mbembe, for example:

Both anger and surprise were breathy, fast, and with low pitch on the final phrase. Yet portrayal of anger included fast nods of the head, with eyes rolling and flashing – characteristics not present with surprise (Pike, 1970a:105).

Revill (*Ibid.*, Appendix II) gives further details including a matrix in which the parameters are linguistic signals (phonological, lexical, and grammatical) and nonlinguistic signals (face, hands, head, breath, body), emotion, and social situation. The obligatory or optional presence or absence of features is shown in the cells of the matrix.

Sign language, on the other hand, is not quite the same as the fusion of vocal and gestural behavior. It is, rather, a substitute for speech, a system of gestures which communicates approximately the same content as verbal units and is, therefore, amenable to linguistic analysis. Kakamasu describes the sign language used by the Urubú for communicating with the deaf-mutes of the tribe. He gives a tagmemic analysis of both verbal and sign-language clauses, and points out contrasts and similarities between the two systems. Lexical entries are "spelled" according to combinations of distinctive gestures. The author adds: "The degree of animation in SL [sign language] may add shades of meaning or emotional overtones in a manner similar to intonation in spoken language" (1968:277).

Further such detailed studies of gesture are needed before Pike's hope can be realized for a mathematical approach to gesture which "might conceivably open the door ... to the study of language-speaking human beings – or language formally studied in a context of the formal study of a unified theory of the structure of human behavior as a whole" (1971:96).

1.3. The distribution mode

When trying to define language itself within a model in which part of the definition for all language units is a component of distribution in a larger matrix of some type, Pike came to the conclusion that:

Language is a variety of behavior (not merely a code, or set of symbolic forms, or a mathematical logical pattern).

The distribution requirement forced me to state that language was distributed in culture (1959:53).

Language in its sociocultural setting will be the principal topic for consideration in this discussion of the distribution mode of units of behavior.

1.3.1. *Language in its sociocultural setting*

Bridgeman's analysis of paragraphs in Kaiwa not only illustrates a number of ways in which verbal and nonverbal behavior are inextricably linked, but it is also one of the more detailed studies with respect to the cultural setting of language. The following points are among those treated:

1) Sociolinguistic situations in which different kinds of ethnolanguages and different discourse types occur are described. The ethno-languages distinguished by the Kaiwa are: ancestor speech, Indian speech, and Paraguayan speech [Guaraní].

In one set of situations [religion, indoctrination, and songs] only ancestor speech is appropriate, in another [casual conversational exchange] only Indian speech. Paraguayan speech, though used, is never considered appropriate and its use is often denied. There is some overlap and some subdivision of usage due to age groups (Bridgeman 1966:2).

Bridgeman further notes that:

Determining factors for the use of one or the other ... are more sociological than linguistic the circumstance under which a person speaks, the relationship of the speaker to the hearer, the topic under discussion, and the reasons for the treatment of the topic. The speaker's attitude toward his audience and his topic are marked by paralinguistic features (*Ibid.*:2-3).

One of the main differences in the ethno-languages is the lexicon of each. Although the distinctive words in each co-occur with many "which are common to all three ethno-languages ..., the presence of one versus the other marks the difference in ethno-language and socio-linguistic situation. They are, therefore, not considered to be synonymous nor to be semantic equivalents" (*Ibid.*:94). Consequently, Bridgeman analyzes lexical paragraphs in terms of 1) those which are directly related to the discourse and 2) those which are related to the sociolinguistic situation. Thus, for example, introductory paragraphs "convey the following type of information: the ethno-language which is used, the type of discourse within the ethno--language, and thus the involvement of the speaker with his listeners...; the speaker's role in regard to the theme [and] the relevant lexical domains..." (*Ibid.*:112).

2) Paragraph and discourse levels of structure differ not only in internal construction but also in that paragraphs are distributed into discourse-level tagmemes, whereas discourses "are distributed in a socio-linguistic situation" (*Ibid.:* 62). Conversational paragraphs, however, are frequently "interrupted by short references to events in the socio-linguistic situation", e.g., instructions to children or explanatory asides to a third person in the background or "to acquaint the listener with something in the social situation of which he is unaware" (*Ibid.*:64).

Tagmemic formulas are given for the linguistic representation only of the

contrastive discourse types, but there are descriptive statements of the
sociolinguistic situation. For example:

Indoctrination Discourse is used only under certain formal conditions. The shaman is
dressed in his ceremonial clothes, his lip plug is inserted, he holds a wooden cross in one
hand, a ceremonial rattle in the other. Men who are participating in the ceremony also
wear lip plugs and carry cross and rattle. Men in the audience usually wear lip plugs. The
content is strictly religious (*Ibid.*:12).

Bridgeman mentions also that the audience may repeat the shaman's
statements several times and that the discourse may be interrupted while the
shaman sings to the gods (*Ibid.*:12-13).

Discourse types are further distinguished by the potentiality for participation of speakers and listeners. While ordinarily there is no one present
who does not participate in songs, the Kaiwa believe that the gods are
nonparticipant listeners and are influenced by the songs. Thus, both natural
and supernatural worlds are involved in the event (*Ibid.*:6).

Independent and Sequence sentence types are also distinguished
sociolinguistically: Sequence sentences cannot occur as a complete discourse
but are dependent on some nonverbal behavior (*Ibid.*:23).

3) The sociolinguistic situation in relation to other indigenous groups and the
Portuguese speakers surrounding the village where field work was carried out
is described. The social roles of the informants and their attitudes toward the
different ethno-languages are also well-documented, so that Bridgeman's work
can be taken as a serious effort to describe verbal and nonverbal behavior
within a unified framework.

In a less comprehensive study, Powlison describes the interchange, on one
occasion, between narrator and audience in which the narrator of Yagua
folktales was continually interrupted by questions for clarification or by
corrections. Further data are necessary to confirm whether this kind of
interchange is typical of Yagua folktale narration (1965: 111).

Chenoweth treats music as language since it is "meaningful expression
intelligible within culture" (1969:218). She therefore brings tagmemic
concepts to bear on the analysis of three Duna singing styles. The purpose or
subject matter of each style is delineated, as well as criteria for participation
by various social groups.

Pike and Larson (1964) describe different rhythms in their situational
context: the formalized antiphonal responses between a host group and a
group of visitors, the shaman's chanting, the informal ditties of Aguaruna
women on occasions of excitement, and the stylized pattern in crying, used
by young children and by women in wailing over the dead.[5]

96

Whereas Bridgeman and others writing on different styles include sociolinguistic and other cultural data in their analyses, Scott excludes it. In his analysis of Persian and Arabic riddles as a highly stylized type of literature, he quotes Saporta as mentioning the possibility that literary utterances may be regarded as an overlap between language and art, that is, as phenomena which have a dual membership in these two classes of human behavior. Scott admits that this alternative (among others) is intuitively appealing, "since it leads to the conclusion that the analysis of literary texts is an interdisciplinary activity" (1965:2). Nevertheless, he rejects this view, since it forces the linguist outside "his role and the proper limits of his discipline" (*Ibid.*)

He distinguishes riddles from other genres by contrasting the discourse level tagmemes of riddles with those of other genres. For a study within the tagmemic framework, it is, indeed, curious that he should conclude that the nonverbal, social matrix in which riddles are told is a necessary component of the definition of the genre, but that linguistics cannot describe this (*Ibid.*: 74-75). Perhaps the social matrix can't be described in other linguistic theories, but a basic assumption of tagmemics is that language behavior is a "part of total human behavior, and obtains its structuring *only* in reference to that larger behavior field, and relative to the structural units of that larger field, the linguist must ... refer to that larger field in order to get access to that frame of reference..." (Pike, 1967:68).

Not only does the social context determine in many cases the ethno-language and type of discourse; it also determines when it is appropriate for certain members of the society to speak. Eunice Pike (1969:108) cites the fact that a Mazatec teen-age girl must be kept out of focus, and hence is not permitted to participate in conversation, except under special circumstances. When this is carried over to relationships with outsiders, it may mean that the junior, female member of a team (of linguists, missionaries, etc.) has difficulty finding opportunities to practice speaking the language in socially acceptable situations.

Wise points out that exhortations in Nomatsiguenga should be given only by those of certain appropriate kinship categories, e.g., mother's brother to his sister's child (1971:208). The roles of participants in other speech events are also partially determined by the social setting:

The oldest man, relative to any particular group assembled, is the recognized story-teller and the only one who may appropriately tell myths... Moreover, it is improper at all times for a younger man – say under 40 – to tell a myth (*Ibid.*: 212).

Although primarily oriented within the framework of generative semantics, Grimes' and Glock's article on a Saramaccan travel narrative appears to be influenced by tagmemic concepts. The importance of the social setting is suggested in their discussion of the highly stylized interchange of formal courtesies and proverbs in a court interview. The behavior of participants in the interview is determined according to rank. One participant must have the rank of village chief or higher and "one or two minor participants repeat the speech of the principals to avoid the appearance of direct communication" (1970:422).

Pike (1964b) illustrates the interaction of sociological and behavioral factors in contributing to lexical meaning, hierarchies of inclusion in grammatical constructions, and phonological manifestations of units. Name fusions, growing out of the need to identify single-girl partnerships as social units lead to new lexical particles in which there is not a one-to-one mapping between form and meaning. The "meaning" does, however, reflect some formal elements of individual personal names or surnames.

In an introductory essay on tagmemics, P. Fries illustrates the fact that certain sequences of sentences make sense only when the social situation is understood: "Double function occurs in three general situations. Could I have some cream and sugar, please? These three situations are..." (1972:195). He points out that if one knows this sequence occurs in a restaurant and the second sentence is said to the waitress, then there is no problem of understanding.

This sort of phenomena is treated by Pike (1963a) as a multichannel communication medium, analogous to segmental and suprasegmental units in phonology. He shows that suprasegmentals such as tone sometimes operate simultaneously in a language in lexical and grammatical constructions and that there are subsegmentals, e.g., voice quality, also operating simultaneously. Pike then extends the multichannel communication system to a multichannel system of behavior. Ordinary physical behavior is treated as segmental, while conversation is suprasegmental to it. Subsegmental to these two are the shared orientation and social value systems, constituting a background or matrix within which the physical and conversational activity take place. During a conversation on a particular topic at a luncheon, however, a request like 'pass the salt' is suprasegmental to the inner segmental eating and directly relevant to it whereas the conversation on a topic is not.

Not only must verbal behavior be interpreted in its nonverbal, cultural matrix; the converse is also true. In her introductory guide for learning an unwritten language, Gudschinsky remarks:

Observed behavior cannot be understood [by an anthropologist studying a little-known culture] apart from the verbalizations of participants and local observers... The vast bulk of the culture cannot be directly observed within a single field experience; the investigator is dependent upon anecdotes, explanations, and extrapolations provided by his informants (1967:1).

The concept that language must be viewed within the larger cultural context is inevitable in a theory in which distribution is one of the modes, i.e., kinds of structuring of language. Since the distributional concept of hierarchy (illustrated in Pike, 1967:chapter 3, by a church service) is discussed elsewhere in this volume, it will not be discussed as such in this chapter. We turn rather to some studies dealing more specifically with the cultural matrix of language behavior.

1.3.2. *Cultural studies*

Bock's descriptions (1962 and 1964) of the occurrence of social roles in a "situation matrix bounded by a period of social time and an area of social space" (1964:397) is primarily a nonverbal analogue of verbal behavior. There are, however, important implications for further development of the interrelations between verbal and nonverbal behavior. For example, his studies point out that certain actions, including verbal ones, are appropriate for a participant performing a specific social role, since there are "inter-related behavioral expectations making up any given social role" (*Ibid.*:394). "The *key* to the identification of roles and attributes which underlie them is the recognition of the social space/time matrix (situation) as an integral part of the description... for... the expected interpersonal behaviors which constitute the attributes of roles... function, in part, to contrast 'kinds of persons' " (Bock, 1962:181).

Thus, in accord with classical tagmemics, Bock interprets specific behavior as a manifestation of a role. However, his work departs from tagmemics in that he identifies cultural forms, i.e., social units of role, time, or space, by formal, contrastive-identificational features and gives a fairly rigorous statement of distribution but "does not explain or give the meaning of the Indian Wake [for example]... The aim remains strictly *formal*. Content enters the analysis only for the purpose of contrast" (1964:401).

On the other hand, he does include meaning to the extent that cultural forms [units] are "a set of inter-related, partially arbitrary expectations, understandings, beliefs or agreements, shared by the members of some social group, which can be shown to influence (or to have influenced) the behavior of some members of that group" (1962:156).

In his later work Bock is quite specific that a motivational component is not only unnecessary, but that its absence is advantageous since psychological problems which the structuralist is unprepared to handle are avoided (1967:173).

The other important components of his model are (1) that "role behavior is placed in its space/time context, (2) [the concept of internal structure is adopted making it] possible to describe variants and segments of the role, ... (3) the notion of external distribution makes possible the integration of any given matrix into larger structures" (*Ibid*.) These components should make it possible to describe social structure focussing on "*recurrent situations* characteristic of a society, the situation in terms of which members of that society orient their behavior, through both participation and anticipation" (*Ibid*.).

In his discussion of institutional conflict in relation to social time, the internal structure and external distribution of which he describes in some detail, the limitation of a model which leaves out the purpose of behavior is seen. Bock shows that a model is necessary which gives information "concerning the relative power, decision-making processes and strategies of the groups ... involved [in order to predict how institutional conflicts will be resolved]" (1966:101), but that "a structural analysis which yields a formal statement of the *units* and the *relationships* (of time, space, and social action) ... [is] prerequisite to ... more process-oriented (functional) explanations" (*Ibid*.:102).

In another role-oriented study, Franklin hypothesizes that the "manifestations of the C[ultural]-tagmemes are various linguistic and/or symbolic speech characteristics associated with the cultural role at some level in the society" (1970a:170). While thus illustrating the inseparability of verbal and nonverbal behavior, he appears to limit cultural tagmemes to social roles and the verbal behavior associated with them and not to recognize that there are some cultural units which are not necessarily manifested by speech characteristics. His limitation of the cultural tagmemes to social roles may arise from the fact that any tagmeme is a correlation between a function (grammatical and/or situational role) and a manifesting set, coupled with the fact that he posits the individual as the lowest level of the cultural hierarchy.

Similarly, in an article on eliciting cultural data, Franklin seems to limit a unified analysis of verbal and nonverbal behavior to a correlation of the social roles of individuals "with the grammatical expressions related to the roles" (1971:345). Although his concept of societal tagmemes seems to be much more limited than the theoretical potential, the value of his suggestions for eliciting cultural material should not be under-rated. Some of his examples for eliciting the purpose of a particular pattern of behavior and for finding terminology appropriate to a specific universe of discourse are especially helpful.

Pike makes suggestions for further tagmemic cultural studies:

> The behavioral setting within which any one activity hierarchy (or unit thereof) occurs is a complex of such hierarchical composites of activity ... a NETWORK OF INTER-WOVEN HIERARCHIES of activity. The activity of one fan or one player [in a football game] provides one component of the larger activity...
>
> If, now, the individual genealogies of two hundred randomly selected individuals from a small community were separately plotted and then superimposed one on another, the composite chart would symbolize an intricate network of partially overlapping relationships... (1967: 117).

The tagmemic concept of matrices, with intersecting dimensions of contrastive categories, coupled with the concept of matrix conflation, should be particularly applicable to interwoven, overlapping networks of activity or of role relationships. As far as I can determine, however, Bock's work is the only application to date of matrix techniques to cultural studies. (Cf. Pike and Erickson, 1964, for discussion of matrix conflation in morphology studies and Pike, 1964b, for analysis of name fusions via matrix techniques.)

1.3.3. *Language and cultural change*

Unfortunately, there have been few detailed tagmemic studies in the area of language and cultural change and diversity. As Ornstein notes in his introduction to a proposal for viewing linguistic change within the tagmemic model: "Ironically enough, although tagmemicists have been predominantly anthropological linguists, unusually close to multilingual contact points in a number of countries, they have concerned themselves very little with this area of research ⌊language diversity and change⌋" (1972).

He comments further that while no one theoretical model has been designed with a view to accounting for patterned variation in language, neither does any theory exclude *ipso facto* investigations of variability and that "the linguistic or sociolinguistic variable has been extremely influential in providing a viable bridge between linguistic and social phenomena" (*Ibid.*).

Ornstein's primary concern is to develop a marking system which would provide information on the sociolinguistic constraints upon the use of linguistic features or items. He accomplishes this primarily by the use of subscripts in tagmemic formulas which indicate that a form is a variant and information in parentheses indicates its status, e.g., (S, in)='standard, informal'.

With regard to language diversity, Pike notes that speakers of a language from different social strata may have somewhat different but topologically related systems with a few points where one has extra phonemes or

morphemes, over-differentiation, etc.[6] Variations in individual and
geographical dialects and change over time are also treated as topologically
related (1967:582). "That set of component units of a series of dialects –
whether social, geographical or temporal – which are topologically related ...
comprise the OVER-ALL PATTERN or COMMON/CORE" *Ibid.*:583)[7]
Elements not related topologically are considered to be COEXISTENT
systems (*Ibid.*).

In a brief statement on change and bilingualism, Pike again refers to the
notion of common core, i.e., units shared between dialects, but refers also to
a larger matrix:

All structural change occurs over a 'bridge' composed of a unit shared (1) by two
systems, or (2) by a sequence of units larger than the shared unit.

A shared unit implies the presence of a larger system embracing the two systems. The
larger system constitutes an interaction matrix (1960b:1-2).

He further differentiates between nuclear and marginal shared components,
including geographic zones which are nuclear to one language or the other
and the transition zone between them where bilingualism is more likely
(*Ibid.*:3).

In one of the few tagmemic descriptions of language change, Saint and
Pike document a case of extreme phonological change and distortion and
subsequent return to the phonetic norms of Auca in the case of a teen-age girl
who was isolated from other speakers of the language for several years.

The intonation was drastically altered ... In addition ... the characteristic Auca voice
qualifiers (principally the use of faucalization, of laryngealization, and of occasional
phrases spoken with indrawn breath) which give dramatic effect were lacking.
    Specific segmental distortion also occurred .. (1962: 27-28). By comparing recordings
made at different stages, the authors note:
    Within a matter of days or weeks after she was joined – still outside the tribe – by
two of her aunts, the voice qualifiers and intonation were normalizing.

    Now, two full years later, all phonemic contrasts and distributions seem to be
restored, although a few traces of her former distortions still remain (*Ibid.*:29-30).[8]

Elsewhere, in commenting on linguistic and cultural change, Pike again
emphasizes the shared components:

The dynamics of change in time is the dynamics of waves of movement of one system to
another system with indeterminate areas between ... One system does not cease and
another one begin with a gap between them ... And yet all is not transition in a single
"flat" sense. Rather there are periods and peaks when certain items or certain phases of
systems are prominent" (1959:50). (Cf. also Pike, 1961:267.)

Franklin applies the concept of shared components to the religious dedication services of church-buildings in Kewa — a ceremony begun in the process of acculturation — and to the indigenous ritual in which a head man recited a spell while opening the door to a particular spirit house as part of a healing ceremony (1971:345).

Chenoweth and Bee categorize Awa songs according to topic and/or occasion of performance and indicate which social groups — of age or sex — may sing each. They comment that the functional significance of the song types may change through time or be lost completely. War songs, for example, have become obsolete since warfare has been virtually abolished in the area, while many other songs "are relegated to the sing-sing dance after their functional significance diminishes" (1971:774). The authors, therefore, do not consider dance songs to be a special category.

Wise (1970) cites a case in which a system of kinship terms has changed, apparently within the last 50 years or so, from symmetry to asymmetry in ego's generation. The obsolete symmetrical usage is retained in at least one legend and also occurs in one biographical narrative of events occurring about 50 years ago. Whether or not there have been accompanying changes of nonverbal behavior has not been investigated.

Hymes (1969) urges Pike to extend the actual scope of tagmemic studies, since *Language in Relation to a Unified Theory of the Structure of Human Behavior* promises an open-ended exploration of cultural behavior which has not been fulfilled. Inasmuch as few tagmemic works can be cited in the area of nonverbal behavior, one must conclude that Hymes' point is well taken. It is hoped that such an extension will be forthcoming in the not-too-distant future.

2. MEANING IN BEHAVIOR

In contrast to some other current theories, e.g., generative semantics and stratificational grammar, in tagmemics all emic units of behavior are considered to be form-meaning composites: "the present theory forces the rejection of any theory which sets up emes of meaning — i.e., sememes" (Pike, 1967:187). The concept that human behavior is structured in form-meaning composites is reaffirmed in this chapter also, although it will be seen in sections 2.3. and 2.4. that there are alternative views as to which aspects of structure should be considered form and which meaning.

In this section attention will be given primarily to the meaning aspect of language, focusing primarily on the functions of language behavior and the kinds of meaning communicated, but it will again be demonstrated that language cannot be separated from nonverbal behavior. Nida stated a decade ago (but not within the tagmemic model): "Languages are basically a part of culture ... This being the case, the most fruitful approach to the semantic problems of any language is the ethnological one" (1964:97). Emphasis on meaning is, therefore, both necessary and appropriate in discussion of a theory in which linguistic and sociocultural phenomena are treated within a single unified framework. Pike and Pike suggest:

Meaning, in part is (i) the abstraction of the *intent* of the speaker ... Disjunctively, however, meaning is definable (ii) as also including the *impact* on the hearer – his *understanding* and his *behavior* ... An adequate translation should retain the *focus* of attention of the speaker, along with (or part of) his intent (n.d.:10.12).

Within tagmemics, then, meaning includes not only the referential aspect of communication but the speaker's attitude as well. P. Fries draws attention to the fact that language may function also to establish social contact or to fill awkward silences once social contact has been made (1972:196).[9]

Various enumerations of the functions of language have been given by theoreticians interested in interpreting speech events in terms of purpose. Hymes lists seven: "1. Expressive (Emotive); 2. Directive (Conative, Pragmatic, Rhetorical, Persuasive); 3. Poetic; 4. Contact; 5. Metalinguistic; 6. Referential; 7. Contextual (Situational)" (1972:117). Halliday, on the other hand, lists three which he considers to be components of meaning, all of which are "normally present in an adult utterance" (1970:326). They are: "the 'ideational' or content function, the 'interpersonal' or social role function and the 'textual' or discourse function" (*Ibid.*)

In this section three functions of language, each of which is considered to be a component or aspect of meaning, will be discussed:(1) those having to do with the observer as speaker, including the I-thou relation as the basis of all communication (section 2.1.); (2) sociocultural context, including social roles (section 2.2.); (3) referent or content (section 2.3.). The section concludes with a consideration of interrelations between these aspects of meaning, including a discussion of some relevant discourse factors and alternative models for showing interrelations between form and meaning.

2.1. *Observer meaning*

The observer as speaker adds aspects of meaning in addition to the referential message he communicates. These include focus on a particular part of the referential meaning, indication of his degree of involvement and the speaker-addressee relation.

2.1.1. *Focus of attention and degree of involvement*

In initial discussion of focus, Pike used the analogy of photography: as the photographer can vary height, depth, and breadth of focus, so the observer may focus attention narrowly on one individual in a narration or he may note details in depth, give a breadth of background information, etc. A football game is discussed as a detailed illustration. (1967:98-119).

As a consequence of variations in focus, accounts of the same event may differ greatly. Thus, in contrasting the four Gospels, Wallis states:

So-called parallel passages differ in their *internal structure*, according to the purpose of the author who selects and slants certain events.

Each Gospel reflects a consistent individual *independence* of focus ..." (1971:4).

She holds that the Gospels can be distinguished on the basis of the differences in focus. As a consequence of this difference, she posits a different discourse role of Christ in each with a consequent emphasis on different groups of His enemies. (Cf. also Wise, forthcoming, on observer viewpoint in the selection and distribution of information from the same "real world" situation, i.e, from the same referential meaning, and on subordinate vs. coordinate grammatical constructions as possibly meaning that the speaker is giving more attention to one event than the other by subordinating the less important one, and that they are both given the same attention in coordination.[10]).

Some studies have dealt particularly with the observer's focus of attention on different participants:

Powlison's "Paragraph analysis of a Yagua folktale", (1965) is early example of a linguistic analysis which highlights the focal role of certain participants by drawing attention to the grammatical devices which indicate who is in focus.

The speaker's focus of attention on a participant who is neither speaker nor addressee but rather a 'topic' in a narrative is described by Frantz for Blackfoot. The use of third, fourth, or fifth person forms is dependent on focus. A speaker may shift focus by using a third person form to refer to a new character, or he may maintain it on the same character who was in focus in a previous sentence by using a fourth person form to refer to a new character even if the focal character is not referred to overtly in the sentence (1966:51).

Pike (1964a) and Wise (1971) treat focus of attention in relation to situational, i.e., referent, roles of participants. (For discussion of these studies, see section 2.3. That same section also mentions a number of other studies in which relations between focus and situational role are discussed.)

According to Wheeler's analysis of Siona, the speaker's focus of attention on a particular participant is one of the factors in the choice of nominal affixes which at first glance seem to be simply surface structure case markers. Nonlinguistic behavior by the speaker provided important cues in the initial stages of analyzing this system of affixes which, as it became evident, indicate not only the role relationships of participants but also emphatic focus, normal focus, or nonfocus. In sentences where the role relationship is ambiguous, it is resolved by the context of discourse or by the social situation.

Degree of involvement of the speaker is the decisive factor in the choice between moods in Siona. Thus, for example, "Siona women talk about their own children's behavior using the definite involvement construction and switch to the indefinite detachment in referring to an outsider's children" (*Ibid.*:72). The speaker's viewpoint of an event as "pertinent to present 1967: circumstances or no longer of any significant application" (*Ibid.*:73) is the important factor in tense so that there is some overlap in actual time:

The immediate constructions apply to events which have recently happened, very seldom longer than three weeks previous. The distant constructions may be applied to events as recent as a week, but generally longer ...(*Ibid.*)

Whereas choice between moods indicates degree of speaker involvement in Siona, Wise shows that for Nomatsiguenga Campa the use of the passive voice at certain points in legends indicates an uninvolved attitude on the part of the speaker, i.e., he is reporting a story as he heard it and is not himself focusing attention on one or another participant. In Nomatsiguenga Campa, as in the closely related Machiguenga, first or second person passive forms do not occur nor can they be elicited. This constraint is adduced in support of the hypothesis that the meaning of passive in these languages is 'speaker uninvolved' (1971:5).

The speaker's emotion, i.e., the expressive function of language, is another facet of observer meaning.[11] Braun and Crofts sketch the features of voice quality and "vocalization − voice qualifier of intensity, extent and pitch height" which express the speaker's mood or emotion in Mundurukú (1965:35).

In his consideration of patterning in oral reading of poetry, Pike treats impact and appropriateness as elements of meaning. Furthermore, he argues that there are elements of creativity supplied by both the writer and the reader, but that the writer should have the freedom to indicate the kind of intonation and other elements of style which he intends as part of the meaning of a poem (1970b).

2.1.2. *Speaker-addressee relation.*

Turning now to the speaker-addressee relation in the speech event and, following Pike (1973:158), we posit this "I-thou" relation as the basis for all communication and agree that "meaning has reference to COMMUNI-CATION between individuals" (Pike, 1967:598). Although the basic concept remains unchanged, this is one area in which there has been considerable recent development of the tagmemic model, especially in the formal treatment of conversation.

In pursuing the fundamental importance of the "I-thou" relation, Wise describes some parts of Nomatsiguenga Campa narratives which are related to the speech event rather than the narrated event itself.[12] For example, a story may begin 'now yesterday," i.e., 'now [I'm going to tell you what happened] yesterday' (1971:153-154). She adds:

> Monologue is normally embedded in dialogue ... Greetings and farewells ... were part of the larger context in which the recording [of monologue speech] was made. Greetings and farewells are not only a part of the more inclusive dialogue within which monologue occurs; they are also a way in which the speaker-addressee relationship of the particip-ants in the speech event is established (*Ibid.:* 207).

In delineating the features which distinguish various compound propositions, i.e., which distinguish different relations between propositions, Wise and Green (1971) posit speech event and narrated event as the most inclusive contrastive categories in the dimension of contrast having to do specifically with relations between propositions, while reportive vs. interpretive observer viewpoints are posited as the other dimension of contrast.

Stout and Thomson describe a "shell" — introduction and coda — and "plot" in Kayapó narrative. They point out that the "shell" relates the plot to the occasion of telling. Speaker attitude is usually revealed in an evaluative section between the complication and resolution sections of the plot (cf. Labov and Waletzky, 1967). In addition, explanatory paragraphs give "the narrator's personal ideas or experiences" (1971:252).

Although Klammer's work is primarily on the structure of dialogue paragraphs, some aspects of it fall within the scope of this chapter, since he adopts the tagmemic view that language is "a variety of behavior, with no sharp discontinuities allowed analytically between verbal and non-verbal activities ... We allow non-verbal as well as verbal units of behavior to manifest Sp[eech] function-slots" (1971:11).

The most important way in which his work is related, however, is in the emphasis on the primacy of dialogue in all of language as communication. Klammer holds that "the question-response system and the interactional relation between two or more persons upon which it is based are fundamental units within any cultural system" (*Ibid*.:54).[13] Or again, "The dialogue relationship between two human beings ... is the *sine qua non* for the existence of language [and] not only underlies all of linguistics, but is also the foundation upon which the very possibility of human social interaction depends" (*Ibid*.:341).

Accordingly, he posits dialogue as clearly more basic than monologue and considers monologue as, in fact, involving a speaker and addressee(s). Even in soliloquy there is an audience (in theatrical soliloquy); "in life [they may be] thought of as dialogues with oneself" (*Ibid*.:36).

Klammer further points out that social conventions control all dialogues. "Kings and commoners, fathers and sons, professors and students all must follow cultural rules that determine what may happen in their dialogues" (*Ibid*.:35). (Cf. sections 2.2. and 2.4.) In addition, he relates special kinds of dialogue to the social situation in which they occur, e.g., notes passed at a meeting (*Ibid*.:40).

2.1.2.1. Formal treatments of conversational rules. Several recent studies deal more specifically with conversation as such, and in work by Pike and Lowe several aspects of conversation are formalized within the framework of mathematical group theory. (Pike's and Lowe's studies are, for the most part, limited to three participants, whereas Poythress [1973] gives a formalism to handle n-person conversational sequences.)

Beginning with his first applications of group theory to linguistic problems, Pike (in Pike and Lowe, 1969) insisted that a formalization be sociologically relevant, so that sociolinguistic phenomena would be displayed explicitly and generatively. Lowe, in proposing an algebraic theorem to account for English pronominal reference in conversation, states that along with distinguishing exclusive and inclusive plurals, "conversational sequences, distinguishing socially acceptable ones from the unacceptable" (1969:399) must be accounted for.

Pike (1973) deals more specifically with sociological factors in conversation. He gives different formal representations of pronominal axes and shows that the well-formedness of conversational sequences differs sharply in accordance with the situation. Hence, the formalisms themselves cannot be evaluated except by criteria outside the formalism; when sociolinguistic criteria of naturalness are applied, the most natural turns out to have interesting mathematical properties as well:

Two mathematical models, each of which can generate precisely the same terminal strings, may carry radically different sociolinguistic consequences in relation to larger discourse structures ... The difference between some generators can show up only after the second stage of a conversational interchange (*Ibid.*:149).

Differences between structures are not detectable within any one single recorded conversation, but only (a) as a deduction from the sum of all available conversations, or (b) by the use of negative information, where informants reject certain paths — certain possible conversations — as being unacceptable (*Ibid.*:151).

In addition, rules of courtesy are given in some detail within the group theory treatment. Pike adds: "It is cues such as surprise (or anger, or reprimand) that let us know when a culturally sanctioned, mathematically representable conversational sequence has been broken" (*Ibid.*:127).

Lowe (1973a) affirms that the conversational sequences which correspond to the universals of reply to speaker, and to switches of addressee (generator elements of the group), are the most natural and can occur in almost unlimited social situations. In contrast, the social conditions under which other sequences may occur are more limited and these, in fact, correspond to non-generator elements of the group.

In Lowe (1973b) these ideas are further developed and used to explain the usage of 'come' versus 'go' in English. The model is generalized to include cases when encoding time and place, i.e., the speech event, are not identical to time and place of the narrated event.

Pike shows that the simple group, i.e., the generator elements of the group and the relationships between them, is applicable (1) to control of pronominal reference in monologue exchanges between three persons in discourse; (2) to identification of referents in direct quotations, and (3) to analysis of change of roles in a narrative as a whole and in its paragraphs (see Wise and Lowe, 1972). He then adds:

Human behavior — including language behavior and its structure — includes complexity so great that, in order to represent it naturally, a complex mathematics must be used ... But on the other hand, for the least effort in human behavior, one may want minimum building blocks. Therefore I propose: ... the combination of complexity obtainable by using a non-commutative group, plus the simplicity (or least effort) obtainable by repeated use of the minimum non-commutative group, makes the six-group, non-commutative, a logical candidate for repeated use in modeling human behavior (1973:157).

In order to show the importance of the minimum commutative group and its relation to the minimum non-commutative one, Pike reaffirms that "every narrative, conversation, or discourse must have, as prerequisite to it, either the explicit or implicit 'I-thou' relation which is mapped by the I generator of the I,r group" (*Ibid.*:158).

With regard to language acquisition, he adds:

The minimum situation in which the 'I-thou' relation might conceivably be learned is in a discourse situation of two parts: utterance and response ...

But this may still be too simple. It may turn out that a child, to learn 'I-thou', must be one of a minimum of three persons, so that the full set of six axes is available for comparison (*Ibid.*:159).

2.1.2.2. *Performatives*. While tagmemic theory does not deal with performatives as abstract predicates in the same sense in which they are treated in generative semantics (cf. Ross, 1970), Pike states specifically: "Within a particular discourse, each relation such as 'you to him' or 'he to someone other than you or me' or 'he to me' must ultimately be related to an 'I-thou' relation from which they are derived by the group operations (or extensions of them) given here" (*Ibid.*). That is, pronominal reference is conceived of as controlled by discourse speaker-addressee roles rather than being generated from recursive nodes. (Cf. section 2.4. for discussion of discourse roles as controlling factors of situational roles, i.e., roles of arguments, in the sequence of actions in narrative.) Pike continues:

We must *not* assume, i.e., that each sentence in a discourse is somehow related *independent of the other* sentences of that discourse, to an 'I-thou' relation underlying that sentence alone. Instead, the discourse as a whole relates them all in one generative package ... It is the total chain of statements and quotations which must be traced backward to find the effective group index of any one part.

Thus the whole underlying structure of pronominal relations with [sic] a discourse as a whole must include as a starting point the identity element, corresponding to the 'I-to-you' axis (*Ibid.*:158-159).

In tagmemic theory, then, a "performative" 'I say to you' is posited on the level of a monologue discourse as a whole, whereas in most generative semantic treatments an underlying performative is posited for each sentence. For example, Pike (1973:158, fn.26) quotes Sadock as proposing a speaker-addressee relation in an abstract proposition underlying every sentence in the language and assuming that "Sentences are THE [emphasis added by Pike] tools of communication, and hypersentences are responsible within the theory of transformational grammar for this utility" (Sadock, 1969b:343). The different views as to the level of structure at which performatives should be posited can probably be attributed to preoccupation with the sentence in transformational grammar as opposed to the tagmemic idea that "the abstracting out of sentences for study is a legitimate and useful procedure ..., [*but*] it is a deliberate distortion introduced in order to handle the data" (Pike, 1967:484).

Wise also (1972a) suggests that in a narrative text, an underlying 'I say to you' should be posited on the discourse level rather than each sentence of it.

The fact that modals occur at paragraph-like intervals in Nomatsiguenga, but in each independent clause in Cashibo, and, further, that other phenomena related to the speech event occur at certain prescribed points in a discourse, is cited to support the hypothesis that although languages differ in the surface-structure placement of modals, performatives should not be posited for every sentence of a discourse.

The whole subject of performatives should cause one to question the validity of the *la langue: la parole* and competence: performance distinctions. Although performatives are treated as abstract predicates in generative semantics and, therefore, discussed as part of the linguistic competence of the speaker, they are, nevertheless, *speech acts*. It would seem to me inevitable that discussion of speech acts should eventually lead to a consideration of the performance of those acts without a rigid distinction from abstract considerations of competence.

2.2. Social meaning

Social meaning, which often is not made explicit in a message, is communicated through implicit presuppositions, shared values, and the social relations between participants in both the speech event and the narrated event. Although there is no clear line of demarcation between social meaning and the I-thou relation of observer meaning, in section 2.1. we were concerned more with the latter, since it reflects the individual speaker's viewpoint, whereas here we shall be considering primarily the social relations between speaker and addressee and their shared presuppositions and values in a particular sociocultural context. (Other kinds of social meaning, including social roles of participants, will be discussed in section 2.4.)

2.2.1. *Presuppositions.*

In discussing meaning in the lexical hierarchy, Pike and Pike comment that there is "a *social* cumulative sharing, in which a set of words with their usages (and implicit or explicit definitions) is passed on from father to son" (n.d.:14.6). They point out also that there are "specific constraints imposed by the fact that the speaker and hearer have particular biographies, experiences, and social settings" (*Ibid*.:14.2-13).

While tagmemic discussions have not normally used the term "presuppositions" the notion of culturally defined conditions of appropriateness and of understanding have been an integral part of tagmemic theory. Universe of discourse, situational context, and sociocultural context are some of the tagmemic equivalents of "presuppositions"

Klammer defines universe of discourse as:

The whole system of shared assumptions and experiences that enable speaker and hearer to communicate and which determine the understanding they will have of the verbal and non-verbal units they employ ... The universe of discourse is determined anew for each pair of participants in a dialogue, ... [so that it is] an ad hoc system which nevertheless has constant parameters associated with the dialogue roles of speaker and hearer. Within a universe of discourse, units are form-meaning composites (1971:33-34).

Pike (1964c) shows that the effectiveness of some kinds of literature hinges on the fact that there are pivotal elements which cross over between two universes of discourse, often by homonymy. "Double-voiced discourse" and parables are also examples of a function of language in which a great deal or most of the meaning is missed if the total situation is not taken into account. In double-voiced discourse there is, in addition to the referent, a hidden polemical attack against another speech act on the same topic (cf. Klammer, 1971:42-43).

In a brief article pointing out the metaphorical or parabolic nature of songs sung at the dance grounds of a Kewa clan, Franklin delineates some of the social significance of the songs. The total social context, including warring between clans and the fact that the songs allow "traditional enemies to let off steam, without cutting off heads" (1970b:990) makes the social, parabolic meaning much more important than the referential meaning. Of particular interest is the fact that in accommodating to the special phonology — musical rhythm and timing — actors, goals, and location are often obscured, thus making it possible to insult indirectly the guest clan which listens to the performance. Paralleling "common Kewa narrative" style in which a speaker may represent several actual actors, the songs may implicate a whole clan but are sung as if only one man were speaking (*Ibid.*:989).

Sarles, in his article on questions and responses, discusses presuppositions in dealing with context or situation.

The Q-R system inherently involves a relationship between two (or more) *persons*, who must implicitly share a sense of what the question *and* response 'mean' in any particular context.

Particular questions occur in 'real' situations which are culturally relevant, and which partially define an answer as 'correct' or not (1970:83).
Actual sentences take place in actual contexts, where much of the context is so clear, obvious, and shared, that it need not be — and is usually not — discussed *out loud*. It appears to be no less a part of that sentence, however, than if it had been said.

> In context, then, sentences may well occur – but may also include for their
> understanding or interpretation the information which is present in the situation
> (*Ibid.*:85, fn.3).

In a recent stylistic analysis of a newspaper article, Hutchings points out that "whatever information the author wishes to impart in this article, he must impart against a background of certain shared assumptions" (1973:91). While the body of his study is not overtly tagmemic, Hutchings concludes by observing that there are three phases of analysis of the text: 1) isolation and labelling of features, 2) observation of these features as dynamically functioning units, and 3) observation from the wider sociocultural context. He further suggests a correspondence between these phases and Pike's particle, wave, and field. Hutchings emphasizes that "any text ... is a social event taking place within a cultural tradition" and that "there are aspects of the meaning which cannot be accounted for by reference to the text alone" (*Ibid.:* 94).

Some transformationalists, particularly some of those working in generative semantics, are also beginning to acknowledge that "there are areas of linguistic competence that cannot be described in any theory that does not allow an integration of information about the context in which the discourse takes place" (R. Lakoff, 1972:909).

Furthermore, as is the case with performatives, it seems that consideration of presuppositions and related concepts is leading inevitably to a less rigid distinction between competence and performance. Garner, for example, relates presuppositions to performance: "A speaker who presupposes does not do so as a performer of a sentence act token, but in the performance of an illocutionary act (or the purported performance of one)" (1971:42).

Grimes, working within the framework of generative semantics, but with considerable tagmemic influence, seems to recognize that performatives and presuppositions are related to verbal behavior in its larger cultural context rather than to the abstract competence of the speaker. He comments that the recognition of performatives "paves the way for linguistic handling of situational factors in discourse [including deictics and personal pronouns]" (1972:90). He further states that indirect discourse reflects the actual speech situation, since person assignments are taken directly from the performative that dominates the entire discourse.

Grimes considers speaker viewpoint to be a presupposition and comments that the speaker's decisions "including the relations among them are referred to as the underlying formational structure (since it is verifiable only indirectly from the forms he utters and the *behavior* [emphasis mine] that is associated with the uttering)" (*Ibid.*:37). (Cf. also G. Lakoff, 1971, on presuppositions.)

Keenan, writing within a generative-transformational framework, is quite specific in relating presuppositions to the utterance or performance of sentences while at the same time showing that presuppositions are independent of truth value.

Now many sentences require that certain culturally defined conditions or contexts be satisfied in order for an utterance of that sentence to be understood (in its literal, intended meaning). ...These conditions include among many others: (a) status and kind of relations among the participants; (b) age, sex, and generation relations among the participants; (c) status, kin, age, sex, and generation relations among the participants and individuals mentioned in the sentence; (d) presence or absence of certain objects in the physical setting of the utterance; and (e) relative location of participants and items mentioned in the sentence itself.

Once these particular relations have been elucidated we might hope for a general definition of *appropriateness* of an utterance in a context. Then we could state the general definition of pragmatic presupposition as follows: An utterance of a sentence presupposes that its context is appropriate (1971:49).

2.2.2. *Characterizations and appropriate behavior.*

In tagmemics, the concept of appropriateness is not limited to utterances in context. It is relevant also in those sociocultural contexts where certain actions are understood as typical of participants having certain roles. identification of participants in discourse is then possible even in cases where nouns do not occur and there are no formal cues. Duff (1973), for example, cites a case in Amuesha where the agent of an action can be identified, by a native Amuesha, as the shaman since it is an action typical of shamans. She points out that in translating material unfamiliar to the Amuesha the agent, goal, etc., must often be made explicit since the reader will not always know which actions would be appropriate for roles foreign to their culture.

Wise (1971:95-96) discusses such phenomena as characterization of participants. (Bock also dicusses the fact that certain actions are appropriate for participants performing certain roles, cf. section 1.3.) Grimes, who discusses actions appropriate to a particular character, in his section on performatives, further elucidates this point:

Characterization involves providing information about a character, either by talking about him descriptively or by reporting selected actions he performs. This information must be given in such a way that when the character comes to do something that has particular significance in the plot, it will be then be [sic] plausible for him to do it because it is consistent with what else is known about him ... Characterization ... depends heavily on the richness and accuracy of the speaker's assessment of who the hearer is and what his background is (1972:19-20).

Appropriateness and characterization may also be treated as selectional restrictions between actions and participants as well as between actions and the case frames or roles of their arguments:

> One kind of selectional restriction is seen in the fact that it is characteristic of the Leader in Pre-Andine Arawakan cultures to 'own' the dam constructed by all the members of a fishing party. In languages such as Amuesha where nouns occur rarely and third person pronouns are not distinguished for gender, the owner of the dam is never in doubt to anyone knowing the culture, even though the form is 'third person's dam' (Wise, 1972b).

The behavior appropriate between certain pairs of kin is also one of the concepts shared by members of a society. The way in which the kinship terms reflect social roles of participants, and help to identify them when personal names are not used, is pointed out by Wise (1969). Furthermore, when there is a choice of terms the use of one over the other reflects certain values held by a society. For example, in Nomatsiguenga Campa, the father of a young girl usually refers to his wife as 'the mother of my daughter' rather than 'my wife', reflecting a kind of social organization in which there is matrilocal residence with some bride service expected. "When a man has a marriageable daughter who will soon bring a son-in-law to help with the work, he is more likely to refer to his wife by the form which stresses her role as the girl's mother" (Wise, 1971:6). Another example is seen in Kayabí where spirits can be referred to only by third person pronouns and the dead are referred to only in whispers because of the shared beliefs of the members of the society (Rose Dobson, manuscript).

2.3. Referential meaning.

In this section we turn our attention to reference or the specific message communicated. Plot, as referential meaning in folklore, and clause-level roles of participants (in any discourse type), e.g., agent and goal, will be the main topic of discussion. Pike and others have referred to these roles as "situational roles", "meaning of grammatical tagmemes", "case", "sememic structure", etc. The relation of these roles to behavior and some alternative views as to where they fit in the tagmemic model will be discussed in section 2.4.

2.3.1. *Plot as referential meaning in folklore.*

In discussing meaning on the discourse level, Pike and Pike state:

Two or more stories can have the same (or similar) tree structure with radically different plots (meanings). Although a unit must have both form and meaning as a composite ..., the two can vary independently (n. d. : 2-8).

Dundes seems to advocate a similar view of plot in folklore and follows Propp in considering that a given action cannot be defined apart from its function in the total narration. He modifies Propp's approach with some concepts from tagmemics and provides a formulaic description of the narrative action of folktales. Actions, defined as motifemes, are taken as the stable, emic units and the characters who perform them as variables leading to allomotifs. Folktales are then defined as sequences of motifemes so that the motifeme is seen in its distributional context (Dundes, 1962 and 1963).

In a subsequent article (not necessarily in a tagmemic vein), Dundes shows the necessary relation between the study of folklore in literature and the study of folklore in culture and that in either type of study the cultural and literary contexts are important. He gives an interesting example of a "mistake" in the narration of a folktale which shows that the narrator identified himself with the Indian boy in the story (1965:141).

Horner (1968) does not specifically allude to Pike or the tagmemic model, but his motifemic-slot-sequences, posited as the patterning of folktales, appear to be very similar to a tagmemic treatment.

Although not attempting to follow Propp and Dundes in all details, Wise posits discourse or chapter-level roles of participants in folklore and describes the order in which they are normally introduced. If the villain is not introduced first, then the role of the one who is introduced first is made quite clear in the opening sentences of a folktale (1971:150-151).

Functions, or discourse-level tagmemes, similar to those of Dundes, are suggested also. It is noted that the etic order of functions in a folktale, i.e., the surface order in which a story is told, does not always follow the same pattern. In the chronological order, however, reflecting the emic, underlying plot-structure, the order of functions remains the same in different versions of a tale (*Ibid.*:152-153).

2.3.2. *Clause-level roles of participants.*

In the first exposition of tagmemics, the clause-level, situational roles were included:

John runs home. John has been hit in the eye... John is tired. At least some of these sentences must be considered as beginning with separate gramemes [tagmemes] because of the sharp differences in their structural meaning and proportion (... actor-as-subject versus recipient-of-action as subject) ... Nevertheless, there is some kind of distributional unity among them ..." (Pike, 1954:131).

This proposition was in sharp clash with the linguistic climate at the time. For example, in commenting on positional meaning, Pike (1954:150) notes that C. Fries (whose work had a strong influence on Pike) insists that "such terms as 'subject,' 'indirect object,' 'direct object' have no relation to the actual facts of a situation in the real world" (*Ibid.:*175). Unfortunately, most tagmemic articles ignored the distinction between actor and subject, and referred merely to "subject". In discussing Philippine languages, Pike is more explicit on the need to show the "relationship of each tagmeme to the real world, in addition to its grammatical function" (1964a:7). In those languages it is necessary to discuss voice or focus relationships as well as "situational" roles such as agent, instrument, etc.

Pike says that by the voice relationship in Philippine languages:

> The hearer is informed that the observer's (or speaker's) attention is oriented toward the relation between the action of the predicate and its actor, or ... its goal ... In each of these types the physical event – the etic situation, the denotation – is constant, and signalled by the transitivity of the clause. But the emic focus – the directed attention of the observer (or speaker) to one of the relations of the activity as reported – becomes contrastive (1963b:217).
>
> Pike distinguishes focus from emphasis as follows: Focus reports the observer's attention to one of several relations – without essential emotional overtones – between a predicate and some other part of a clause ... In emphasis ... some one substantive is singled out for a direct isolated overlay of emotional connotation without formal (emic) reference to a dependence upon its relation to the activity to which it is in (etic) fact related (*Ibid.:*219).

To accomodate situational role, focus, and emphasis as independent variables he utilizes the concept of simultaneous, i.e., portmanteau, manifestations of tagmemes so that a given nominal expression may simultaneously manifest actor-focus-emphasis, instrument-emphasis, etc. Tagmemic studies of Philippine languages on situational role and focus include the following:

Forster (1964) considers the topic-comment relation, i.e., focus in Pike (1963b and 1964a), to be a binary, immediate-constituent structuring of clauses which is superimposed on the string-constituent structuring seen in the relationships between a verb and the nominal expressions in it.

Lee, who rejects the notion of a binary, immediate-constituent structure in Maguindanao, discusses primarily the nature of units with non-focused verbs and proposes that they also be considered clauses, redefining clause as "a string composed of a verb and substantive phrases (including focused and non-focused items)" (1964:53).

Newell gives a fairly extensive discussion of situational roles in relation to grammatical roles for Batad Ifugao and points out that "a narrative clause always states the course of an action (either causal agent or actor)... [while] a descriptive clause ... does not ... unless it is focussed as the topic of the clause" (1964:182-183).

Kerr (1965) gives a rather comprehensive treatment of "voice" and "case" in Cotabato Manobo and compares the structures briefly with those of other Philippine languages. His use of the term "case" for the relationship between the verb and nominal expressions seems to refer primarily to surface structure. Nevertheless, his discussion relates the cases to the "situational roles" of the participants, although he does not use the term. He further gives detailed discussion of "voice" relation between the the verb and one of the nominal expressions.

If a given nominal expression is topic its case-like relationship to the verb is not marked in the topic expression itself ... but in the verb by the voice affix. If the nominal expression is nontopic, its case-like relationship to the verb is marked in the nominal expression itself (*Ibid.*:16).

The voice focuses the relationship of the nominal expression to the verb, and the topic has priority on focus over other clause-level nominal expressions.

Shand (1964) relates focus and tense to problems of verb morphology. On the other hand, Morey (1964) relates focus and aspect not only to verb morphology but also to phrase, clause, and discourse levels of structure. In the verb morphology co-occurrence restrictions between aspect and focus markers are discussed in detail. Reid (1964) also deals primarily with morphological forms – the noun phrase rather than verb forms – in relation to topic or focus and situational roles.

Dan and Marilou Weaver (1964) relate questions of grammatical role and topic to the forms and sequences of tagmemes manifested by personal pronouns in Agusan Manobo. The topic set of pronouns occurs before the source set which in turn occurs before the oblique set. Furthermore, the speaker outranks the hearer who in turn outranks any third person.

Miller (1964) relates situational roles, grammatical roles, and focus to verb stems in Mamanwa. Ward and Forster point out some inadequacies of this treatment and classify Maranao verb stems in transitive clauses according to whether or not instrument, etc., are optional or obligatory. They qualify this, however, with the statement that "in a well defined linguistic or cultural context, the participant in the event does not have to be specified in a given clause provided it is clearly understood otherwise (1967:42, fn.7).

Following in the same vein, but in an article not explicitly tagmemic, Hall (1969) classifies Siocon Subanon verbs according to the inherent and transfer features of each. The latter specify the situational roles implied for each of the participants. He then shows the relations that match situational roles with grammatical cases.

In a later statement of the distinction between grammatical functions and situational roles, Forster and Barnard (1968) assume a situational hierarchy which is distinct from the grammatical hierarchy:

> The situational string of an active verb includes the action described by the verb, the participants directly and indirectly involved in the performance of the action, the setting of the action in time and space, and optionally such things as the reason for the action, the means of performing the action, and the distance covered when the action involves motion... [Some] such as causer ..., beneficiary ..., objective (that which is included in the action, often in a subordinate or incidental way) are only indirectly involved in the performance of the action, and can be said to be optional in their occurence with the verb. There are four participants directly involved in the action of active verbs ...; actor ... goal (that acted upon), instrument ... and site (that toward or from which the action is directed).

> There are four clause level grammatical slots ... relevant to our classification of Dibabawon active verbs – subject, object, associate, and referent. Each of these ... can potentially function simultaneously as the topic of the clause; the focus inflection of the verb identifies its function as subject, ... A classification of Dibabawon verbs based on the grammatical slots occurring in the clause or on the potential focus of the verb is not adequate without some reference to the underlying situational string because verbs which can occur in the same grammatical construction do not necessarily occur in the same situational string, and vice versa (*Ibid.*: 266-267).

In a study of Eastern Otomi of Mexico, Voigtlander and Bartholomew (1972) analyze the situational roles permitted with different verb stems, distinguishing these from the morphological constructions permitted for each stem. The treatment includes mapping via the lexicon so that it shares certain assumptions with stratificational grammar as well as tagmemics.

Bee does not seem to distinguish situational roles from grammatical roles but, in general, her functional slots seem to be situational roles, e.g., she carefully distinguishes goal from direct object (1973:73). She does not discuss the fact that the same situational role may have more than one surface form and vice versa. Her distinction of means, instrument, and manner (*Ibid.*:76), according to whether or not the clause is action or condition oriented, seems to be quite useful.

Becker (1967a and b) applies the distinction between situational roles and grammatical roles to English subject tagmemes. The former are considered to be grammatical meaning and the latter grammatical form (cf. section 2.4. for further discussion of this point). He shows that in rules of conjoining, "a phrase of the same type" must be interpreted to mean having both the same grammatical role and the same situational role.

J. Platt (1971) also discusses the interrelationships between situational roles and grammatical forms. He discusses location in detail and distinguishes nuclear location, which is closely related to one of the situational roles of participants, from outer, non-nuclear location [not seen].

Hale (1973) and Trail (1973) [not seen] give extensive examples of clause-level analyses in which situational roles are posited as the meaning of tagmemes. These studies reflect work by Pike and Hale, and by Becker (cf. Pike and Pike, n.d.; Hale, 1972, and Becker, 1967b).

The roles currently posited by Pike, Hale, and Trail are limited to agent, undergoer, and site or scope, so that they are similar to roles of arguments in generative semantics and do not so closely reflect actual situational roles as a treatment in which more roles are posited. Undergoer, for example, is more or less equal to "objective" in generative semantics: the complement of an event such as 'see', 'make', 'begin', try', etc., is considered to be undergoer, in addition to the "patient" of an event, such as 'hit'. Actor and undergoer are relatively specific roles, while scope or site may be one of a variety of situational relationships.

<h3 style="text-align:center">2.4. Interrelations between observer, social and referential meaning.</h3>

2.4.1. *Interrelations illustrated.*

Interrelations between observer, social, and referential meaning are illustrated by Pike (1968 and 1970a) for Bariba:

> The cultural setting, the focus of attention, and sequence of pronominal reference are heavily interwoven in the structure of direct versus indirect discourse (Pike, 1970a:57).
> Of several characters ... one may be out-of-focus. The character out-of-focus is quoted indirectly whereas the character in focus [who is likely to be the chief] would be quoted directly (*Ibid.*:62).

While Pike's study shows how choice of direct or indirect discourse is affected by interrelationships between the three kinds of meaning, other recent studies discuss the referential, social, and focal roles of participants in discourse and show how the three kinds of roles are interrelated.

Wise (1970) summarizes a Nomatsiguenga Campa legend in which the victims are changed into another form by the villain in the conflict unit of each chapter. In the mediation unit someone intervenes on behalf of the victims, and in the resolution unit the villain is changed into another form. In this and other legends, as well as in legends from the related Amuesha language, the characters are referred to by their kinship roles, indicating something of their relation to one another in their society. These roles are interrelated with the villain, victim, and [hero] mediator roles in that those who side together are parallel relatives, while those who are against each other are cross relatives. The role of the baby's mother, however, is ambivalent toward the villain, her brother, whom she saved from being burned along with his co-villain at the close of the second chapter. As the conflict in the third chapter develops, her role as the mother of the baby (victim and cross-nephew of the villain) becomes more important. In that role she is on the opposite side from her brother.

It is further pointed out that the speaker's focus of attention is also interrelated with the plot roles and social roles. This interrelation is shown in that kinship roles are expressed in terms of a character's relation to the participant who is the focus of attention.[14] In the third chapter, for example, the villain is the focus of attention. Therefore, the anguished mother says, 'He [i.e., my brother] turned his cross-nephew into a rock on me' rather than *'He turned my baby into a rock'. Thus:

... social roles, plot [referential] roles, and focal roles ... are all closely intertwined and only partially autonomous. All three must be considered for a complete understanding of the part each character plays (*Ibid.*).

Another example of the interrelationships of the three kinds of roles is seen in Nomatsiguenga Campa person-marking affixes. Normally the distinction between masculine and non-masculine third person forms and between singular and plural enable the hearer to identify the referent in a more-or-less straightforward manner. However, at certain points in a discourse, in which a group of participants work together, their social roles control number: the singular form occurs and refers to the particular participant who is the initiator of the action of the whole narration. On the other hand, choice of gender sometimes indicates focus of attention: a mixed group of participants is ordinarily referred by the masculine third-person prefix, plus the plural suffix. If, however, the non-masculine third-person prefix occurs, it indicates that the observer's focus of attention is on a woman who is part of the group (cf. Wise, 1971:67-68 and 90).

Larsen illustrates for Ancash Quechua some ways in which social roles are related to plot roles in legendary discourse. The place in society of the leading character is established in the introductory, background section of a narrative. His role often gives a hint of the type of conflict which he will have to resolve. "Other characters are usually referred to with a noun phrase which indicates their kinship relation to him" (1970). If a character other than the protagonist is in focus for one part of the discourse, reference to other characters may indicate their kinship relation to the one temporarily in focus. "A character with a very minor role, however, frequently retains the original kinship reference" (*Ibid.*).

In their analysis of *Little Red Riding Hood*, Klammer and Compton point out the interaction of Social Setting with Observer Viewpoint and Plot in the use of 'Mother' and 'Grandmother' which "reflect directly the social situation in which these participants function in the narrative ... [whereas] LRRH is called 'LRRH' and not 'Daughter', ... since the observer (the narrator) ... is focusing on and viewing events in relation to LRRH" (1970:219).

They further point out that the "grammatical formula 'Once upon a time there was ...' ... indicates not only the usual fairy tale setting in the indefinite past ..., but also the backgrounding of the person of the narrator with a resultant freedom ... to focus upon and see things in relation to the main character" (*Ibid.*).

Although these three kinds of roles are interrelated, they are, nevertheless, independently variable: the social leader, for example, is not always the focus of attention. Furthermore, focus and social roles, such as initiator, are relative to the speaker's viewpoint and the social situation. Wise cites an example from Nomatsiguenga Campa which occurs in a set of stories about a plane trip, each told by the same narrator but from the viewpoint of a different participant:

[In the sentence 'I caused her to fly' the initiator or causer] ...may be the pilot of the plane if he is speaking... Or, the initiator may be a nurse taking a patient by plane for medical treatment if the nurse is speaking. Or, he may be a man taking his little daughter along with him on a plane trip. In the last two cases neither the nurse nor the man piloted the plane, but with relation to the patient the nurse initiated the trip and with relation to the daughter the father initiated the trip (1971:116).

2.4.2. *Interrelated roles in sequence of actions in narrative.*

For a more complete understanding of the interaction of these roles it is necessary to consider structures beyond the sentence. Pike (1964a) mentions the necessity of exploring how "situational roles" are related to grammatical roles and how these are related to discourse structure. He further shows the need to specify the sequence of situational roles performed by the participants in a story from one sentence to the next and suggests that there may also be a restriction on the kinds of grammatical constructions which can occur in sequence.

In addition, Pike points out that not only can there be variation in the lexical items which represent a participant in a given situational role, but also that the same situational role can "migrate" (*Ibid.*:14) to slots on grammatical levels other than clause. He suggests eliciting a story from different viewpoints in order to "find out how observer viewpoint affects the flow of situational roles ... and the flow of constructions through the discourse" (*Ibid.*:10).

Wise, building on Pike's suggestion, describes the sequence of roles in a Nomatsiguenga Campa fishing story and calls attention to the fact that "the appropriate sequence of roles is an important cue to identification in discourses where there are multiple third person participants [and few nouns]" (1971:161[1968:243]).

In a subsequent study, Wise and Lowe (1972) show more specifically that the situational roles of participants in a given action are dependent on their discourse roles which remain stable throughout the story. In a simple autobiographical narrative these are primarily social roles such as leader (initiator) and follower(s) (helper). The sequence of situational roles is described by means of group theory.

Barnard and Longacre posit three discourse-level participant roles in Dibabawon game-procurement narratives: initiator, objective, and props. These roles remain constant except in parenthetical, peripheral, or embedded constructions: the initiator, for example, is actor or causer on the clause level, while the objective is the goal (1968:197).

Another example in which the social roles of participants remain relatively constant throughout a discourse is cited by Bradley (1971) in her discussion of Jibu narrative-discourse structure. The structure, which is also described by means of mathematical group theory, is somewhat more complex than in the Nomatsiguenga Campa fishing story. A priest acts for the initiator at certain points and on other occasions he and the initiator act as a single group in interaction with the responding group. These roles are related to the situational roles, i.e., cases, of participants in individual actions of the story. The permutations are based on a hierarchy of these cases — Agentive, Experiencer, Goal, and Objective — which define who has the initiative and who is responder in a given instance. (Cf. Grimes, 1971:95, for ranking of roles as tantamount to a scale of relative involvement in actions.)

A development beyond the work of Wise and Lowe is Bradley's description of expansion of the group playing the responder's role in the reversal permutation of the first section and the narrowing of that group in the reversal permutation of the final section.[15] In the second section the attitude of the narrator changes, so that he does not include himself: "either the narrator is so disgusted with the proceedings that the dissociates himself from them, or else he was outside dancing, while the main characters were meeting" (*Ibid*.:9).

Grimes also discusses participant orientation, i.e., participant roles in the sequence of events in a narrative. Nomatsiguenga Campa is apparently different from the languages which Grimes considers in at least one aspect of orientation: in Nomatsiguenga the patterned sequence in which participants perform certain roles is not apparent at all in the linear, surface structure of a narrative; rather, the story must be rearranged in chronological sequence for the pattern to emerge (cf. Wise, 1971 and 1972a). Grimes, on the other hand, analyses orientation in the linear order; he states: "It is quite possible that the sequencing of role sets is related to Chafe's notion of postsemantic shaping (1970), which results in a derived semantics that is not too different in its structure from the surface or output form of discourse" (1971:94, fn. 3).

2.4.3. *Alternative models for showing interrelations.*

We turn now to consider some alternative tagmemic models for interrelating the three kinds of meaning with each other and for interrelating "situational roles" with grammatical roles.

In the model proposed by Pike and Hale (see section 2.3.2.) situational roles are considered to be part of the situational or sememic structure of clauses, and the grammatical roles part of the organizational structure. Only three nuclear situational roles are posited. While three or four roles or arguments — e.g., agent, objective, experiencer, and referent, proposed by some generative semanticists — may be adequate when verbs are lexically decomposed into one or more logical predicates, they do not seem to be adequate when verbs are not decomposed, as is the case in the Pike-Hale model. Recently when B. Newman and I were studying Longuda clauses (unpublished manuscript), we found certain verb classes which seemed to us to be associated with different situational roles. The classes also differed in their potential to enter into various sets of derived constructions, e.g., causative and stative, but could not be distinguished in their internal structure using only the three roles posited by Pike. A larger set of roles, more closely reflecting actual situational relationships, would have enabled us to account more adequately for the differences in derivational potential. Limiting ourselves to three situational roles did not seem to afford much more insight into the structure of Longuda clauses than that gained by consideration of surface-structure grammatical roles only.

For some purposes, however, a limited set of roles or classes of roles is necessary. In the Wise and Lowe study of Nomatsiguenga Campa, the sequence of roles did not emerge clearly until speaker, agent in non-causative clauses, and causer were classed as "agentive" in "that the participant having [one of] these roles takes the initiative in the action" (1972:14). Addressee, beneficiary, referent, agent in causative clauses, and co-agent were classed as "dative" in that they "share the feature that the participant having [one of] these roles does not take the initiative" (*Ibid.*). Similarly, goal and attribuant were classed together as "objective" since they "share the feature that the participant is affected by the action or state of the action" (*Ibid.*:15); and purpose, instrument, and location were classed as "oblique", a less direct relation to the action. While lexical decomposition is not explicit in the Wise-Lowe study, nor in Wise's work (1971 and 1972a), neither are deep-structure propositions equated with surface-structure grammatical clauses. Consequently, grouping of certain roles in classes should not be equated with the three roles of the Pike-Hale model where grammatical and situational features comprise a single form-meaning composite. Delineation of the optimum set of roles for studies within the tagmemic framework is, I believe, an unfinished task.

Roles which are implicit in certain verbs pose a different problem. In Nomatsiguenga Campa, for example, 'coca', an "undergoer", is implicit with the verb *monga-* 'to chew' but never occurs overtly. Only when something else, e.g., chewing gum, is the object, and hence the undergoer, is this role explicit. Pike and Hale do not discuss such cases. Perhaps they would be handled as a clause with an undergoer situational role but zero object, or as portmanteau action-undergoer as situational role of the predicate.

Nor is it clear how a set of expressions such as 'I have fear' (a transitive clause), 'fear is with me' (an intransitive clause) and 'my liver is yellow' (a descriptive clause), (example adapted from data supplied by B. Newman for Longuda), each of which has the same situational relationships, would be handled in this model. They are all paraphrases of the meaning. 'I am afraid', but it appears that they would have to be handled as members of separate clause types with no means of showing the relation between them. The Pike-Hale approach seems to require that one start with form — the surface verb form and the noun phrases associated with it — at least for analysis and presentation. The reverse — starting with meaning — does not seem to be possible, although it should be in a theory in which all units are form-meaning composites.

Pike and Pike state that this model with only three situational roles "allows specificity for actor and undergoer, without losing a degree of expandability [in the nonspecific scope role] to cover other kinds of relations, without which a language could not serve old or developing social needs without proliferating the number of formal roles into an unmanageable size" (n.d.:4.17). This last statement seems to imply that there must be a different grammatical role for each situational role, a requirement which appears to me to be untenable and to contradict Pike's treatment of lexical units. If more than one meaning or "sense" is allowable for a morpheme, that is, a many-to-one relation between form-meaning composites of the lexicon, why not in the grammar also? Morphological matrices in which there is an "interplay of various one-to-many and many-to-one relationships of formatives [form] to category [meaning]" (Pike and Erickson, 1964:212) provide another example, within tagmemics, where there is no requirement that the number of forms and meanings be the same.

In addition, the use of the term "structure" for both the situational aspect of clauses and for the organizational or formal aspect (cf. Pike and Pike, n.d.:11.24-25) appears to conflict with the concept of the tagmeme as a form-meaning composite. It would be more consistent to consider the total composite as a structure.

The model is based on Becker's proposal of a four-aspect tagmeme (which he attributes to Pike's suggestion), displayed in Figure 1. This view of the tagmeme "reveals two basic tagmemic assumptions: 1) that all grammatical units are form-meaning composites and 2) that tagmemes are correlatives of syntactic slot and lexical filler"

	Grammar	Lexicon
Form	A (e.g., subject)	C (e.g., noun phrase)
Meaning	B (e.g., agent)	D (e.g., single male human, etc.)

Figure 1
Aspects of grammatical units (Becker, 1967b:6).

Pike later (1972) expanded the four-aspect tagmeme to a nine-cell array, as seen in Figure 2. It is not quite clear whether this array is intended to represent different aspects of a single tagmeme or whether it represents separate grammatical, situational, and phonological tagmemes. If the latter, then the model implicitly denies earlier assertions that phonological structures, as well as grammatical and lexical structures, are form-meaning composites.

In this model lexical structures are considered to be specific instances of grammatical and situational structures. Thus, the specific item, e.g., 'the boy' is a lexical entry in the grammatical row, while it is encyclopedic in the situational row, that is, it refers to a specific boy, e.g., 'Ted, son of Mr. Joe James of 420 Sixth Street'. Pike notes that the referent may be the same

	Functional slot, or role	Category, or constitution	Specific item or instance
Grammatical	e.g., subject	[grammatical-con-struction category] e.g., noun phrase	[lexical entry] e.g., the boy
Sememic or situational	e.g., agent [actor]	e.g., animate	[encyclopedic] e.g., Ted, son of Mr. Joe James of 420 Sixth Street
Phonological	[stressed position as phonological slot], e.g., ... ´...	e.g., CV CVV	e.g., /ðə bóI/

Figure Figure 2
Pike's nine-cell array of tagmemic features (1972).

while the specific lexical entry may be radically different, e.g., 'John ... that rascal'.[16]

Another nine-cell model was proposed by Wise (1971[1968]) in which a different relation is posited between "situational" roles and grammatical roles and between "situational" roles and nonverbal behavior.

Before discussing this model the nature of the relation between "situational" roles and the nonverbal behavior to which they refer will be considered. Pike seems to imply that "situational" roles reflect the actual roles of the participants as seen in the citation above (Pike and Pike, n.d., 4:17) and in an earlier statement: "Recent development of space-time role matrices of Philip Bock ... describing anthropologically many of these kinds of components in a sample specific social situation may eventually help define situational roles for tagmemic discourse analysis" (Pike, 1964a:21, fn.12).

If these roles reflect the actual situation, then it seems clear that the role structure of each situation will be culture specific rather than universal. Consider, for example, the situation in which a man has a stick in his hand and uses it to hit a donkey. The referent aspect of meaning is a universal, but the cultural view of the situation is not the same in all languages. In English and Nomatsiguenga, to name languages from different families, the man does something to the donkey with the stick, i.e. it would be quite natural to say 'the man hit the donkey with the stick' (with the roles being man-actor, donkey-undergoer, stick-scope). In Trique, on the other hand, the man does something to the stick on the donkey, i.e., 'the man applied the stick to the donkey' (with the roles being man-actor, stick-undergoer, donkey-scope [data supplied by Bruce Hollenbach]). In some languages of West Africa the relation between the man, stick, and donkey would be expressed something like, 'the man took stick; hit donkey' (Pike, 1970a) (with the roles being man-actor, stick-undergoer, donkey-undergoer).

Furthermore, not only does the cultural context affect the way in which referential meaning is expressed, but the speaker's viewpoint also enters in. Suppose the English speaker wishes to put special emphasis on the stick as the instrument of hitting. In that case he might say 'the man used the stick to hit the donkey' — yet another set of roles.

A further example in which the roles are not the actual situational roles was provided by Bruce Hollenbach (private communication): Imagine a situation in which a man does not wish to take the blame for a dented fender. He may in that case say to his wife: 'I don't know what happened; the car just ran into the tree'. "In this situation the man is [clearly] the agent in the referential meaning, but the observer meaning — in which he refuses to take the blame — impinges upon the referent, so that the car is said to be the agent" (Wise, forthcoming).

It seems clear from these and many other examples which could be adduced that the so-called "situational" roles may, in fact, be different from actual roles in the nonverbal behavioral situation. In the model proposed by Wise (1971 and 1972a) referential roles — more or less equivalent to Pike's situational roles — are posited. (See Figure 3 for a diagram of the model.) These interact with observer viewpoint and social roles, such as initiator, in the culture-specific context, so that the roles ascribed to the participants may be quite different from their actual roles in the nonverbal situation. For example, in the case of meteorological phenomena the actual roles are the same whether they are described in English or an Amerindian language. However, the roles ascribed are not necessarily the same: In Amuesha, 'it rained' is expressed simply as *wahta*, i.e., the verbalized form of rain, whereas the related Nomatsiguenga Campa expression is *opariake anani* 'fell rain'. Here, rain is viewed culturally as a thing which can behave as a person — at least in some actions such as falling. In English the dummy subject 'it' is most commonly supplied in 'it rained'. 'Fall' is not normally used except when the expression is modified, e.g., 'the rain fell heavily for half an hour'.

I consider an event and the appropriate set of roles with participants performing them — the set being determined by the behavioral situation referred to, observer viewpoint, and the sociocultural context — to be a lexemic clause, i.e., a kind of deep-structure proposition. The relation between lexemic clauses and grammatical clauses is not necessarily one-to-one. All three Longuda-like expressions cited above, for example, may manifest the experiential lexemic clause 'I am afraid', but each manifests a

Aspects of form

	Lexemic	Grammatical	Phonological
Observer viewpoint	Ritual greetings to establish speaker-addressee basis of communication	Feminine plural to indicate focus of attention on a woman in a mixed group	Low, impersonal voice quality in Amuesha ritual greetings indicating the observer is not emotionally involved
Reference	Participant's name identifies him clearly Logical and chronological order Information exchanged in ritual greetings	Masculine vs. feminine and singular vs. plural contrasts in pronominal forms help identify participants Linear, surface order	Idiolectal phonetic differences, mimicked in quotations, identify participants
Socio-cultural context	Ritual greetings function as prayer-chant to the sun god, reinforcing cultural values	Singular rather than plural to point out social roles of leader and followers Special grammatical forms of prayer in Amuesha ritual greetings	Special intonation patterns of prayer in ritual greetings

Aspects of meaning

Figure 3

Interrelations of form and meaning. Illustrations having to do with identification of participants are given in the upper part of cells, while illustrations from Amuesha ritual greetings are given in the lower part.

different grammatical clause — one transitive, one intrasitive, and one descriptive. In others words, in Wise's model a "situational role" — i.e., the deep structure role resulting from the interaction of referential, social, and observer meaning — is not considered to be the meaning of a grammatical tagmeme, but the function of a lexemic tagmeme, as seen in Figure 4.

	Function	Manifestation
Grammatical Unit	A (e.g., subject)	C (e.g., noun Phrase)
Lexemic unit	B (e.g., agent)	D (e.g., single, male, human, etc.)

Figure 4
Grammatical and lexemic units (Wise, 1971:24).

In this model form-meaning composites are retained in that any of the expressions which may manifest a lexemic clause or other lexemic (deep structure) construction are considered to be "allo-lexes" of a lexeme. The notion of functional slot and filler class is also retained; a lexemic agent slot, for example, is normally filled by an animate participant. Fillers, however, are not necessarily "lexical"; instead lexical items, i.e., morphemes, are considered to be the lowest level of the grammatical hierarchy. (See Wise, 1971:119-120, 123-129, and 137-138, and Klammer, 1971:75-76 and 83-95, for fuller exposition of contrasts between lexemic and grammatical constructions.)

The difference between this model and the Pike-Hale-Becker model is crucial within discourse where it has been shown that there is an appropriate sequence of situational roles of participants (cf. section 4.2.2.). This sequence, which is the chronological sequence rather than the linear, surface order of a narration, would not emerge clearly if events and the "situational" roles of participants involved in them were not treated separately from grammatical clauses. Such treatment does not appear to be possible when situational factors are considered to be the meaning of surface, grammatical constructions.

The Pike-Hale-Becker model and that proposed by Wise, and somewhat modified by Klammer, have received more attention within tagmemics than have other models for relating language form to nonverbal behavior. Recently, however, Blansitt, in discussing encoding and decoding processes, has moved toward a semi-stratificational model. He cites hesitation phenomena, for example, in arguing for an ordered relation in moving from semology to grammar to phonology: "A realistic explanation of hesitation phenomena is that they are used to allow semantic elements to move through the encoding process" (Blansitt, 1973:11). His paper is one of the first within tagmemics to focus on encoding and decoding – an important area of verbal behavior. The model proposed points up the need for more study in the area of relations between the hierarchies. Is a straightforward mapping from one to the other, as Blansitt proposes, possible? Or, must the hierarchies be understood as simultaneous and interlocking? (Cf. Pike, 1967:565-597; Wise, 1971:212-219, and Wise, 1972a; and Klammer, 1971:87-107.)

I should like to reemphasize that a direct mapping from meaning to sound or even from "situational roles" to grammatical roles, while a desirable goal, is too simple to account for all of the complexities of language. Ritual greetings which take place among Amuesha who haven't seen each other for a while illustrate some of the complexities. These greetings function simultaneously as greetings – establishing the speaker-addressee basis of communication – while at the same time they provide a vehicle for exchange of information about events unknown to the other, and they function as a ritual prayer-chant to the sun god, thus reinforcing shared cultural values. The grammatical forms in these greetings are different from those in ordinary conversation, while low, impersonal voice quality and special intonation patterns also differ from ordinary phonological patterns. These formal greetings, I believe, provide evidence that the three aspects of meaning which intersect with the three aspects of form as lexemic, grammatical, and phonological structures are not linearly related to one another nor can they be mapped from one another in a direct manner. Rather, they must be understood as simultaneous and interlocking in order to adequately account for the complexities of language in its social context.

2.5. *Conclusions.*

As I have attempted to show in preceding sections, consideration of the different aspects of meaning in language inevitably forces the linguist to account for various functions of language and its sociocultural contexts. Most linguists, however, are hesitant to examine these broader phenomena since they are considered to be extra-linguistic, and therefore outside the pale of linguistic inquiry. Fishman's criticism of linguistics is largely correct: "Language 'per se' ... has been examined [by most linguists] for its patterns, as if it were something that existed above and beyond its users and uses" (1972b:7).

One of the goals of this paper has been to show that tagmemics is an exception: it has from its inception insisted that language behavior and social behavior are inextricably interrelated. Some contributions growing out of this unified approach have been discussed in this paper. They include:

1)a theoretical as well as practical framework for studying unwritten, unanalyzed languages monolingually when circumstances demand such an approach;

2) theoretical justification, through the etic: emic distinction, for consideration of native reaction as relevant data for linguistic and anthropological studies;

3) exploratory studies of many aspects of fusion between verbal and nonverbal behavior;

4) studies of language in its larger sociocultural context, including delineation of uses of different ethnolanguages in one case and of appropriateness of behavior in both sequential and social contacts;

5) studies of social role in a space/time situational matrix;

6) formalization of sociologically relevant conversational rules, and subsequent application of the formal group-theory concepts to sequence of role in discourse; and

7) delineation of interrelations between observer, social and referential aspects of meaning.

Let me conclude by sketching some areas which deserve further study and which could be explored very profitably within the tagmemic framework.

1) Fishman mentions that part of the sociology of language "seeks to provide an answer to the question 'who speaks to whom and when and to what end?'" (1972a:2). Bridgeman's study of the occasions when different Kaiwa ethnolanguages are used (1966) is one of the few tagmemic studies which have treated this question in any depth at all, and even her description is far from detailed. Again, Prucha calls for a study "of the social communicative rules of various forms of a particular language code and of some non-verbal codes" (1972:13). Although one finds scattered references to this sort of phenomenon in the tagmemic literature, detailed studies still need to be made. (Note, however, that tagmemics views language as much more than a verbal code.)

2) In-depth studies of gesture and language within a multichannel communication system should add greatly to understanding of communication in general.

3) The potential for studies of language and social change, i.e., emphasis on the diachronic as well as the synchronic, is available in the concept of change over a bridge of shared components. Exploratory studies need to be made to see what new insights are afforded by the tagmemic model.

4) Interrelations between focus of attention of the observer, social roles, and referential roles have been delineated in some detail for one language only. The linguistic community would profit by exploration of these interrelations in other languages.

5) Appropriateness of actions and other presuppositions have been mentioned in several studies but further work is needed.

6) Finally, as Hymes comments:

> Speech cannot be omitted from a theory of human behavior, or a special theory for the behavior of a particular group. But whether we focus on the cognitive or expressive or directive role of verbal behavior, or on the role of speech in socialization, we find a paucity of descriptive analysis of 'ethological studies of speaking in context (1972:130).

The challenge before tagmemics, then, is to develop and exploit its potential as a theory of language — not in the abstract — but of language as speech — as purposeful, communicative behavior which can only be understood in relation to nonverbal human behavior in its sociocultural context.

FOOTNOTES

1 See, for example, Fillmore's discussion of case in relation to tagmemics (1968:88).

2 Goldman–Eisler, speaking as a psychologist, draws attention to the importance of context for psycholinguistics:
> When he [Uhlenbeck, 1963] points out that 'observation of speech-utterances taken out of the actual milieu, is essentially imperfect observation and will lead to linguistically untenable conclusions', when he maintains that 'language is not a selfcontained system ... it functions in its setting, but as soon as a speech-utterance is observed by the linguist outside of its situational setting and as soon as the frame of reference of the speaker is not taken into account, the utterance becomes for him ... ambiguous'; ... Uhlenbeck expresses views which have been fundamental to my own approach to the study of speech phenomena and psycholinguistics (1972:69).

3 Another current theory which shares the assumption that language is purposeful behavior is Halliday's systemic grammar: "Most speech is functionally highly coherent, in the sense that its structure reflects what it is being made to do; and this is what (given just the assumption that speech is purposeful activity) makes it accessible to the learner" (1970:323).

4 In commenting on Pike's rejection of the *la langue: la parole* distinction, Hymes says: "I follow him in assuming that *la parole* has structure also, but I believe the distinction can be usefully retained. Within Pike's system, it can perhaps be treated as a difference in focus" (1972:13ⅰ, fn.12).

5 Another study in which the larger behavioral matrix is considered is Glover's (1969) classification of interrogatives according to both their internal structure and their function. The type of response or lack of it, verbal or nonverbal, is the primary basis for the functional classification [not seen].

Here and elsewhere items listed in Brend 1970 and 1972 or Pike 1966 which appear to be related to the general topic of this chapter but which were not available to the author are listed as [not seen]. Annotations of such items are adapted from Brend or Pike.

6 Fishman also affirms that "language and society reveal various kinds and degrees of

patterned co-variation" (1972b:5).

7 Durbin and Micklin, in a sociolinguistic study based on a transformational model, propose a "group competence" which seems to share some features of Pike's "common core":

An individual's competence allows him to move between various geographical and social dialects. Although his performance would be different from time to time and place to place, he would still have a structural competence which would remain stable in relation to other speaker's competence (1968:324).

8 Nagara (1969) appears to be a detailed tagmemic study of bilingualism [not seen].

9 Scheflen (1965) describes other kinds of communicative behaviors, as well as language, within the tagmemic model [not seen].

10 I am indebted to Robert Longacre (private communication) for the suggestion that subordination is possibly related to focus on one event as opposed to another.

11 Recently transformationalists, also, have begun to give attention to speaker viewpoint. For example, R. Lakoff points out that "particles, like ... *ge* in Classical Greek ... do not add to the 'information content' conveyed by the sentence, but rather relate this information content to the feelings the speaker has about it, or else suggest the feelings of the speaker toward the situation of the speech act" (1972:907).

12 The distinction between speech event and narrated event is adapted from Jakobson (1957).

13 In contrast, Sanders, writing on discourse within the transformational model, posits monologue as primary: " 'Monologue' ... is the domain of formal and referential invariance of first and second person pronouns, and it is actually only in respect to pairs of monologues grouped within the same DIALOGUE that we can properly express the generalizations underlying the correct ordering of questions and answers, or the correct co-occurrences and referential alternations of *I* and *you*" (1970:72, fn.13).

14 This kind of phenomenon was first brought to my attention by Martha Duff in her study of an Amuesha legend (private communication).

15 Wise and Lowe's article was written in 1969, and a copy of the pre-publication draft was made available to Bradley, Grimes, and others.

16 H. Platt (1970) also discusses reference in her treatment of predicates in relation to other clause-level tagmemes [not seen].

17 I am indebted to Eugene E. Loos and Harry Boonstra for many helpful suggestions in the presentation of this paper and to Ann Shanks for her untiring help in the preparation of the manuscript.

REFERENCES

Tagmemic and tagmemic-related studies

Barnard, Myra L. and Robert E. Longacre
   1968   "Lexicon versus grammar in Dibabawon procedural narrative discourse", *Philippine Languages: Discourse, Paragraph and Sentence Structure*, ed. by Robert E. Longacre (=SIL Publications in Linguistics and Related Fields, No. 21), 194-222.

Barnwell, Kathleen
   1966   "Notes on the Mbembe clause system – A preliminary analysis", Appendix I in *Tagmemic and Matrix Linguistics Applied to Selected African Languages* K. L. Pike (1966, first edition of 1970a), 156-181.

Becker, Alton Lewis
   1967a   "Conjoining in a tagmemic grammar of English", *Georgetown Monograph Series on Languages and Linguistics* 20, 109-121.
   1967b   *A generative description of the English subject tagmemes*, Ph.D. Dissertation, University of Michigan.

134

Bee, Darlene L. (ed. by Alan Healey and Doreen Marks)
  1973   *Neo-tagmemics: an integrated approach to linguistic analysis and description* (Ukarumpa, Papua New Guinea: SIL).
Blansitt, Edward L., Jr.
  1973   "Cognitive tagmemics", *Linguistics* 104, 5-14.
  1962   *The social structure of a Canadian Indian reserve*, Ph.D. Dissertation, Harvard University.
  1964   "Social structure and language structure", *SJA* 20, 393-403.
Bock, Philip K.
  1966   "Social time and institutional conflict", *Human Organization* 25, 96-102.
  1967   "Three descriptive models of social structure", *Philosophy of Science* 34, 168-174.
Bradley, Virginia M.
  1971   "Jibu narrative discourse structure", *AnL* 13, 1-15.
Braun, Ilse and Marjorie Crofts
  1965   "Mundurukú phonology", *AnL* 7.7, 23-39.
Brend, Ruth M.
  1970   "Tagmemic theory: An annotated bibliography", *JEngll*, 4, 7-45.
  1972   "Tagmemic theory: An annotated bibliography, Appendix I", *JEngll*, 6, 1-16.
Bridgeman, Loraine Irene
  1966   *Oral paragraphs in Kaiwa (Guarani)*, Ph.D. Dissertation, Indiana University.
Chenoweth, Vida
  1969   "An investigation of the singing styles of the Dunas", *Oceania* 39, 218-230.
and Darlene Bee
  1971   "Comparative generative models of a New Guinea melodic structure", *AA* 73, 773-782.
Dressler, Wolfgang
  1970   "Modelle und Methoden der Textsyntax", *FoLi* 4, 64-71.
Duff, Martha
  1973   "Contrastive features of written and oral texts in Amuesha", *Notes on Translation* 50, 2-13.
Dundes, Alan
  1962   "From Etic to Emic units in the structural study of folktales", *JAF* 75, 95-105.
  1963   "Structural typology in North American Indian folktales", *SJA* 19, 121-130.
  1965   "The study of folklore in literature and culture: Identification and interpretation", *JAF* 78, 136-142.
Forster, Jannette,
  1964   "Dual structure of Dibabawon verbal clauses", *OcL* 3, 26-48.
and Myra L. Barnard
  1968   "A classification of Dibabawon active verbs", *Lingua* 20, 265-278.
Franklin, Karl J.
  1970a   "Grammatical and cultural function in tagmemics", *Kivung: Journal of the Linguistic Society of Papua and New Guinea 3*, 164-175.
  1970b   "Metaphorical songs in Kewa ', *Pacific Linguistic Studies in Honour of Arthur Capell*, ed. by S.A. Wurm and D.C. Laycock, 985-995.
  1971   "Some comments on eliciting cultural data", *AnL* 13, 339-348.
Frantz, Donald G.
  1966   "Person indexing in Blackfoot", *IJAL* 32, 50-58.
Fries, Peter H.
  1972   "Tagmemics", *Language: Introductory readings*, ed. by Clark, Eschholz, and Rosa (New York: St. Martin's Press), 194-208.

135

Glover, Jessie R.
1969   "Structure and function in the Gurung interrogative", *Journal of the Tribhuvan University* (Kirtipur, Nepal) *Special Linguistic Number*, 37-56.
Grimes. Joseph E.
1971   "Participant orientation", *PJL* 2, 93-99.
1972   *The thread of discourse* (= Technical Report No. 1, National Science Foundation Grant GS– 3180) (Ithaca: Cornell University).
Grimes, Joseph E. and Naomi Glock
1970   "A Saramaccan narrative pattern", *Language* 46, 408-425.
Gudschinsky, Sarah C.
1967   *How to learn an unwritten language* (in *Studies in Anthropological Method*, ed. by George and Louise Spindler) (New York: Holt, Rinehart, and Winston, Inc.).
1968   "Análisis tagménico [sic] de unidades que combinan componente verbal y no verbal", *Idiomas, Cosmovisiones y Cultura*, ed. by Fernández Guizetti (Rosario, Argentina: Univ. Nacional del Litoral), 43-53.
Gudschinsky, Sarah, and Harold and Frances Popovich
1970   "Native reaction and phonetic similarity in Maxakalí phonology", *Language* 46, 77-88.
Hale, Austin
1972   "Syntactic matrices: An approach to descriptive comparability", forthcoming in the Proceedings of the 11th International Congress of Linguists.
1973   *Clause, sentence, and discourse patterns in selected languages of Nepal*, SIL Publications in Linguistics and Related Fields No. 40.
Hall, William C.
1969   "A classification of Siocan Subanon verbs". *AnL* 11, 209-215.
Horner, George R.
1968   "A motifemic construct model for the analysis of folktales", presented at the Second Annual International Seminar on Folktale Analysis, Linguistic Institute, Università degli Studi di Urbino, Italy.
Hutchings, Geoffrey
1973   "Discourse in context: A stylistic analysis", *Lingua* 32, 83-94.
Hymes, Dell
1969   "Review of *language in relation to a unified theory of the structure of human behavior*, 2nd edition by K.L. Pike", *AA* 71, 361-363.
Kakamasu, Jim
1968   "Urubú sign language", *IJAL* 34, 275-281.
Kerr, Harland B.
1965   "The case-marking and classifying function of Cotabato Manobo voice affixes", *OcL* 4, 15-47.
Klammer, Thomas Paul
1971   *The structure of dialogue paragraphs in written English dramatic and narrative discourse*, Ph.D. Dissertation, University of Michigan.
Klammer, Thomas Paul, and Carol, J. Compton
1970   "Some recent contributions to tagmemic analysis of discourse", *Glossa: A Journal of Linguistics* 4, 212-222.
Koen, Frank M., Alton L. Becker, and Richard E. Young
1968   "The psychological reality of the paragraph", *Proceedings of the Conference on Language and Language Behavior*, ed. by Eric M. Zale (New York: Appleton-Century-Crofts), 174-187.
Larsen, Helen
1970   "Algunos rasgos distintivos de la narración tradicional en el quechua de Ancash", *Proceedings of the XXXIXth International*

136

Congress of Americanists. , Vol. 5, 29-51. English version, "Some grammatical features of legendary narrative in Ancash Quechua", reprinted in *Advances in tagmemics,* ed. by Ruth M. Brend. (Amsterdam: North- Holland, 1974).
Lee, Ernest W.
1964   "Non-focus verbs in Maguindanao", *OcL* 3, 49-57.
Longacre, Robert E.
1964   *Grammar discovery procedures* (=*Janua Linguarum*, Series Minor, No. 33) (The Hague: Mouton and Co.)
Lowe, Ivan
1969   "An algebraic theory of English pronominal reference (Part I)", *Semiotica* 1, 397-421.
1973a   "Some conversational constraints in crossing social barriers: An algebraic description", presented to the American Dialect Society (Midwest Region), Ann Arbor.
1973b   "The underlying structure of deictic motion verbs in English", presented at the Summer Meeting of the Linguistic Society of America, Ann Arbor.
Miller, Jeanne
1964   "The role of verb stems in the Mamanwa kernel verbal clauses", *Ocl* 3, 87-100.
Morey, Virginia
1964   "Distributional restrictions on co-occurrence of aspect and focus morphemes in Ata verbs", *Ocl* 3, 69-86.
Nagara, Susumu
1969   *A bilingual description of some linguistic features of Pidgin English used by Japanese immigrants in the plantations of Hawaii: A case study in bilingualism,* Ph.D. Dissertation, Universtity of Wisconsin.
Newell, Leonard E.
1964   "Independent clause types of Batad Ifugao", *OcL* 3, 171-199
Ornstein, Jacob
1972   "Sociolinguistic changes viewed within a tagmemic model", *Proceedings of the XIth International Congress of Linguistics.*
Pike, Eunice V.
1969   "Language learning in relation to focus", *Language Learning* 19, 107-115.
Pike, Kenneth L.
1954   1955, 1960 *Language in relation to a unified theory of the structure of human behavior,* Volumes I, II, III (Glendale: SIL). Revised edition, 1967
1955   "Meaning and hypostatis", *Georgetown University Monographs in Languages and Linguistics* No. 8, 134-141.
1956   "Towards a theory of the structure of human behavior", *Estudios Antropológicos Publicados en Homenaje al Doctor Manuel Gamio* (Mexico: Sociedad Mexicana de Antropología), 659-671. Reprinted in *Language in culture and society: A reader in linguistics and anthropology,* ed. by Dell Hymes (Harper & Rowe, 1964), 54-62.
1957   "A stereoscopic window on the world", *Bibliotheca Sacra* 114, 141-156. Reprinted in *With heart and mind* (Grand Rapids: Eerdman's), 35-45.
1958a   "Native reaction", comment in the Proceedings of the VIII *International Congress of Linguists,* 588.
1958b   "Interpenetration of phonology, morphonology, and syntax", *Proceedings of the Eighth International Congress of Linguistics* 363-374; discussion 385-387.
1959   "Language as particle, wave, and field", *The Texas Quarterly 2, 37-54.*
1960a   "Nucleation", *MLJ* 44, 291-295.
1960b   "Toward a theory of change and bilingualism", *Studies in Linguistics* 15, 1-7.

1961   "Stimulating and resisting change", *Practical Anthropology* 8, 267-274.
1963a   "The hierarchical and social matrix of suprasegmentals", *Prac Filologicznych* 18, 95-104.
1963b   "A syntactic paradigm", *Language* 39, 216-230.
1964a   "Discourse analysis and tagmeme matrices", *OcL* 3, 5-25.
1964b   "Name fusions as high-level particles in matrix theory", *Linguistics* 6, 83-91.
1964c   "Beyond the sentence", *CCC* 15, 129-135
1965   "Language – where science and Poetry Meet", *CE* 26, 283-292.
1966   "A guide to publications related to tagmemic theory", *Current Trends in Linguistics, Vol. III: Theoretical Foundations*, ed. by Thomas A. Sebeok (The Hague: Mouton and Co.), 365-394.
1967   cf. Pike 1954, 1955, 1960, *Language in relation to a unified theory of the structure of human behavior* (The Hague: Mouton & Co.).
1968   "Indirect vs. direct discourse in Bariba", *Proceedings of the Conference on Language and Language Behavior*, ed. by E.M. Zale (New York: Appleton-Century-Crofts), 165-173.
1970a   *Tagmemic and matrix linguistics applied to selected African languages* (=SIL Publications in Linguistics and Related Fields", No. 23) (Norman: SIL). Originally published as a report to U.S. Office of Education, U.S. Dept. of Health, Education and Welfare, 1966).
1970b   "Implications of the patterning of an oral reading of a set of poems", *Poetics: International Review for the Theory of Literature*, 1, 38-45.
1971   "Crucial questions in the development of tagmemics – The sixties and seventies", *Georgetown Monograph Series on Language and Linguistics* 24, 79-98.
1972   "Agreement types dispersed into a nine-cell spectrum", presented to the
1973   "Sociolinguistic evaluation of alternative mathematical models: English pronouns", *Language* 49, 121-160.
Pike, Kenneth L. and Barbara Erickson
1964   "Conflated field structures in Potawatomi and in Arabic", *IJAL* XXX, 201-212.
Pike, Kenneth L. and Mildred Larson
1964   "Hyperphonemes and non-systematic features of Aguaruna phonemes", *Studies in Languages and Linguistics in Honor of Charles C. Fries*, ed. by A.H. Marckwardt (Ann Arbor: The English Language Institute of the University of Michigan), 55-67.
Pike, Kenneth L. and Ivan Lowe
1969   "Pronominal reference in English conversation and discourse: A group theoretical treatment", *FoLi* 3, 68-106.
Pike, Kenneth L. and Evelyn G. Pike
n.d.   *Grammatical analysis*, pre-publication draft.
Platt, Heidi
1970   *A comparative study of English and German syntax*, Ph.D. Dissertation, Monash University.
Platt, John
1971   *Grammatical form and grammatical meaning: A tagmemic view of Fillmore's deep structure case concepts* (Amsterdam: North-Holland Publishing Co.) (=Ph.D. Dissertation, Monash University).
Powlison, Paul S.
1965   "A paragraph analysis of a Yagua folktale", *IJAL* 31, 109-118.

Poythress, Vern
1973   "A formalism for describing rules of conversation", *Semiotica* 7, 285-299.
Reid, Lawrence A.
1964   "A matrix analysis of Bontoc case-marking particles", *OcL* 3, 116-137.
Revill, P.M.
1970   Preliminary report on para-linguistics in Mbembe (E. Nigeria), Appendix II
        in Pike (1970a), 115-122.
Saint, Rachel and Kenneth L. Pike
1962   "Auca Phonemics", *Studies in Ecuadorian Indian Languages*: (=SIL of the
        University of Oklahoma, Publication No. 7), ed. by Benjamin Elson
        (Norman: SIL), 2-30
Sarles, Harvey B.
1970   "An examination of the question-response system in language", *Semiotica*
        2, 79-101.
Scheflen, Albert E.
1965   *Stream and structure of communication behavior: Context analysis of a
        psychotherapy session* (Philadelphia: Eastern Pennsylvania Psychiatric
        Institute).
Scott, Charles T.
1965   *Persian and Arabic riddles: A language-centered approach to genre
        definition* (=Part II IJAL, Oct. 1965; *Indiana University Research Center in
        Anthropology, Folklore, and Linguistics*, Publication 39).
Shand, Jean
1964   "Categories and markers of tense, focus and mode in Ilianen Manobo",
        OcL 3, 58-68.
Stout, Mickey and Ruth Thomson
1971   "Kayapó narrative", *IJAL* 37, 250-256.
Trail, Ronald
1973   *Clause, sentence and discourse patterns in selected languages of Nepal and
        India,* (=SIL Publications in Linguistics and Related Fields, No. 41).
Voigtlander, Katherine and Doris Bartholomew
1972   "Semology and transitivity in Eastern Otomi verbs", *Lingua* 29, 38-53.
Wallis, Ethel E.
1971   "Contrastive plot structures of the four gospels", *Notes on Translation* 40,
        3-16.
Ward, Robert G. and Janette Forster
1967   "Verb stem classes in Maranao transitive clauses", *AnL* 9.6, 30-42.
Weaver, Dan and Marilou Weaver
1964   "Ranking of personal pronouns in Agusan Manobo", *OcL* 3, 161-170.
Wheeler, Alva
1967   "Grammatical structure in Siona discourse", *Lingua* 19, 60-77.
Wise, Mary Ruth
1969   "Representación pronominal en Nomatsiguenga (Lengua de la familia
        arahuaca)' *Lenguaje y Ciencias* 34, 1-5.
Wise, Mary Ruth
1970   "Social roles, plot roles, and focal roles in a Nomatsiguenga Campa myth",
        Vol. 5, 125-152 in the *Proceedings of the XXXIXth International Congress of
        Americanists* and in *Advances in Tagmemics,* ed. by Ruth Brend.
        (Amsterdam: North-Holland Publishing Co., 1974), 389-418.
1971   *Identification of participants in discourse: A study of aspects of form and
        meaning in Nomatsiguenga.* SIL Publications in Linguistics and Related
        Fields, 28 (= Ph.D. Dissertation, University of Michigan, 1968).

1972a   "Lexemic structures in discourse", forthcoming in the *Proceedings of the XIth International Congress of Linguists,* 187-196.

1972b   "Some recent advances in tagmemic theory: Illustrations from Amerindian Languages", *Proceedings of the XLth International Congress of Americanists,* Vol. 3, 23-29.

n.d.   "Some contributions of tagmemics to discourse studies", forthcoming.

Wise, Mary Ruth and Harold A. Green

1971   "Compound propositions and surface sentences in Palikur (Arawakan)", *Lingua* 26, 252-280.

Wise, Mary Ruth and Ivan Lowe

1972   "Permutation groups in discourse", *Languages and Linguistics Working Papers* 4,12-34. (Washington Georgetown University Press).

OTHER REFERENCES

Chafe, Wallace L.

1970   *Meaning and the structure of language* (Chicago: The University of Chicago Press).

Durbin, Marshall and Michael Micklin

1968   "Sociolinguistics: Some methodological contributions from linguistics", *Foundations of Language* 4, 319-331.

Fillmore, Charles J.

1968   "The case for case", *Universals in Linguistic Theory*, ed. by Emmon Bach and Robert T. Harms (New York: Rinehart and Winston), 1-88.

and D. Terence Langendoen

1971   *Studies in linguistic semantics* (New York: Holt, Rinehart, and Winston, Inc.)

Fishman, Joshua A.

1972a   *Language in sociocultural change* (Stanford: Stanford University Press).

1972b   "The sociology of language", *Readings in the sociology of language*, ed. by Joshua A. Fishman (The Hague: Mouton and Co.), 5-13.

(ed.)

1972c   *Readings in the sociology of language* (The Hague: Mouton and Co.)

Fries, Charles C.

1952   *The structure of English: an introduction to the construction of English sentences* (New York: Harcourt, Brace and Co.)

Garner, Richard

1971   " 'Presupposition' in philosophy and linguistics", *Studies in linguistics semantics,* ed. by Charles J. Fillmore and D. Terence Langendoen (New York: Holt, Rinehart, and Winston, Inc.), 22-42.

Goldman-Eisler, Frieda

1972   "What should be the methods in psycholinguistics? ", *Linguistics* 89, 68-73.

Halliday, Michael A. K.

1970   "Functional diversity in language, as seen from a consideration of modality and mood in English", *Foundations of Language* 6, 322-361.

Hymes, Dell H. (ed.)

1964   *Language in culture and society: A reader in linguistics and anthropology* (Harper and Row).

1972   "The ethnography of speaking", *Readings in the sociology of language,* ed. by Joshua A. Fishman (The Hague: Mouton and Co.), 99-138

Jakobson, Roman

1957   "Shifters, verbal categories, and the Russian verb", Russian language project, Department of Slavic Languages and Literature, Harvard University.

Katz, Jerrold J. and Jerry A. Fodor
1963   "The structure of a semantic theory", *Readings in the philosophy of language,* ed. by Jerry A. Fodor and Jerrold J. Katz (Englewood Cliffs: Prentice-Hall, Inc.), 479-518.

Keenan, Edward L.
1971   "Two kinds of presupposition in natural language", *Studies in linguistic semantics,* ed. by Charles J. Fillmore and D. Terence Langendoen (New York: Holt, Rinehart and Winston, Inc.), 44-52.

Labov, William and Joshua Waletzky
1967   "Narrative analysis: oral versions of personal experience", *Essays on the verbal and visual Arts,* ed. by June Helm (Seatlle: University of Washington Press), 12-44.

Lakoff, George
1971   "Presupposition and relative well-formedness", *Semantics: An interdisciplinary reader in philosophy, linguistics and psychology,* ed. by Danny D. Steinberg and Leon A. Jakobovits (Cambridge: University Press), 329-340.

Lakoff, Robin
1972   "Language in context", *Language* 48, 907-927.

Nida, Eugene A.
1964   "Linguistics and ethnology in translation-problems", *Language in culture and society: a reader in linguistics and anthropology,* ed. by Dell Hymes (Harper and Row), 90-100.

Propp, Vladimir
1958   *Morphology of the folktale,* trans. Laurence Scott (=*Indiana University Publications in Anthropology, Folklore, and Linguistics,* No. 10).

Prucha, Jan
1972   "Psycholinguistics and sociolinguistics – separate or integrated? ", *Linguistics* 89, 9-23.

Ross, John Robert
1970   "On declarative sentences", *Readings in English transformational grammar,* ed. by Roderick A. Jacobs and Peter S. Rosenbaum (Waltham, Mass.: Ginn and Co.), 222-272.

Sadock, Jerrold M.
1969a   "Super-hypersentences", *Papers in linguistics* 1, 1-15.
1969b   "Hyper-sentences", *Papers in linguistics* 1, 283-370.

Sanders, Gerald A.
1970   "On the natural domain of grammar", *Linguistics* 63, 51-123.

Saporta, Sol
1960   "The application of linguistics to the study of poetic language", *Style in language,* ed. by Thomas A. Sebeok (Cambridge, Mass.: Technology Press), 82-93.

Searle, John R.
1969   *Speech acts: An essay in the philosophy of language* (Cambridge: University Press).

Steinberg, Danny D. and Leon A. Jakobovits
1971   *Semantics: An interdisciplinary reader in philosophy, linguistics and psychology* (Cambridge: University Press).

Uhlenbeck, E.M.
1963   "An appraisal of transformation theory", *Lingua* 12, 1-18.

INDEX

146